MONOGRAPH SERIES

UNITED STATES CATHOLIC HISTORICAL SOCIETY

Volume 36

AN IMMIGRANT BISHOP:
JOHN ENGLAND'S ADAPTATION OF IRISH CATHOLICISM TO AMERICAN REPUBLICANISM

By
PATRICK CAREY

Marquette University
Milwaukee, Wisconsin

Yonkers, N.Y.
U.S. Catholic Historical Society
1982

Office of the Executive Secretary
U.S. Catholic Historical Society
St. Joseph's Seminary, Dunwoodie, Yonkers, New York 10704

To George L. Carey and
Laverne M. Sabers Carey

"I profess in America what I professed in Ireland, and what they who were my associates in Ireland still profess.... I have not changed nor dissembled a single principle, either political or religious, which I have cherished."

(John England to Henry Conwell, 1822)

NOTE ON THE SYSTEM OF BIBLIOGRAPHICAL CITATIONS USED IN THIS BOOK

Throughout this book the reader will find most citations to sources added in parentheses within the text. These will cite the author, date of publication and page references to the source. The "author-date" citations refer to the works listed in the bibliography at the end of the text, where the complete bibliographical citation is provided in a single alphabet. When more than one work by the same author is cited, the titles are listed in order of the year of publication.

CONTENTS

preface

The history of John England (1786-1842) has been told many times before -- most adequately in Peter Guilday's *Life and Times of John England* (1927). England is, however, the kind of intriguing personality and fertile mind that demands repeated historical analysis. As a priest in Ireland from 1808 to 1820 and as an immigrant bishop in the United States from 1820 to his death in 1842, England was nationally prominent in both countries' political and religious movements. In the United States, he was perhaps the most visible and articulate Catholic clergyman of his day. He most effectively represented and articulated, moreover, what was involved in an Irish-Catholic immigrant's adaptation to American political and religious experiences. Furthermore, he greatly contributed to the practical organization and ideological consciousness of the American Catholic minority. His Irish background, immigrant analysis of American principles and practices, creative adaptations of Catholicism to American republicanism, influences upon the formation of Catholicism in America, and his depressing failures to move the American Catholic Church in constitutional directions -- all make England a viable candidate for study in any period of American history, but particularly in the Post-Vatican II era since many of the problems John England faced in the early nineteenth century are plaguing contemporary Catholics: shortage of clergy; demands for lay participation; conflicts of ideologies, personalities, and various immigrant groups; dissensions within the clergy and between the clergy and the laity; and numerous attempts to accommodate the church to American democratic structures. England struggled with all these problems. Some of his solutions were incorporated into American Catholic structures, but others failed to gain acceptance in his own day. His ideological and practical contributions need to be re-examined today; with some accommodation they may still represent live options for the contemporary Catholic community.

These reasons alone make a study of England worthwhile; but there are even more important reasons for another look at England. When Guilday wrote his *Life and Times of John England*, he did not have access to England's writings as a young priest in Ireland. In 1974, I discovered many of these tracts and newspaper writings. They throw new light on his early clerical life and particularly on his political and religious views before he emigrated to the United States in 1820.

Guilday's *Life*, moreover, paid little or no attention to England's ideology. England left us more political and religious publications on both sides of the ocean than any other prominent Catholic immigrant. His thought needs to be exposed more clearly because it explains many of his own practical political and religious programs. By examining England's newly-discovered-Irish works and comparing them to his American writings, this study delineates his thought on the major political and religious questions of his day and describes the effects of different cultural influences upon an immigrant's mind. The book, therefore, recounts how England's mind on political and religious matters evolved, how Irish history influenced that development, and how the American situation conditioned the immigrant bishop's later thinking and pastoral programs. The study examines the historically and culturally-conditioned evolution of England's mind and the effects of this development upon his attempts to adapt Irish Catholicism to American republicanism. Thus, my approach reveals the reciprocal relationship between cultural experience and ideology by showing how an immigrant's changing cultural circumstances affected his thinking and pastoral programs.

One final reason can be given for a new look at England. Historians have repeatedly acknowledged the contributions (as well as deleterious effects) of Irish Catholicism on the formation of American Catholicism in a democratic age; however, an adequate study of the precise influences of Irish Catholic history upon the developments of American Catholicism in the national period remains to be written. The present study makes no comprehensive claims in this regard; rather, it examines the effects of immigration upon a single prominent immigrant, and analyzes the influences of Irish and American circumstances upon

England's contributions to the formation of American Catholic self consciousness and ecclesiastical structures.

My first attempt to analyze England under the above rubric appeared in "John England and Irish American Catholicism 1815-1842: A Study of Conflict," a doctoral dissertation completed for Fordham University in 1975. The present work is a considerably revised edition of the earlier study.

In my research and in writing this book, I have incurred a variety of debts. I am grateful, first, to the United States Catholic Historical Society who offered to publish this study and to Mr. James J. Mahoney, Executive Secretary of the Society, who has given me many useful suggestions in preparing the text; second, to numerous library and archive staffs (acknowledgements given in the bibliography) who generously assisted me on innumerable occasions -- especially to the National Library, Dublin, Ireland and St. Patrick's College Library, Carlow, Ireland; third, to those teachers whose interest, encouragement, criticism and advice have greatly contributed to this study -- I am particularly grateful to Dr. Maurice R. O'Connell, Rev. Francis X. Curran, S.J., and Rev. Sabbas J. Kilian, O.F.M., all of Fordham University; fourth, to Rev. Gerald Fogarty, S.J. of the University of Virginia at Charlottesville, my dissertation advisor, whose guidance during my research and whose repeated encouragement since then have made this study an enjoyable collegial experience. Finally, my greatest debt of gratitude belongs to my wife, Phyllis Knight Carey, who is my best friend and the sharpest yet most sympathetic critic of my writings. She not only shared the enthusiasm and burdens of research in Ireland, but also followed the book through its various stages, helped type different drafts, and provided for our financial support while this work was in progress.

introduction

The French Revolution, among other things, put the European Catholic Church in competition with the principles and practices of religious liberty, separation of church and state, voluntaryism, and republicanism. In the minds of many European Catholic churchmen at least, these principles and practices were equated with the forces of revolution; in the minds of many of the revolutionaries, they were identified with the inevitable march of history and the evolving modern democratic world. To many churchmen, however, they had directly destroyed or at least diminished the church's rightful influence in society. The churchmen, therefore, rejected the principles and saw the "progress" of the modern world as detrimental to the church's welfare. In setting itself against the French Revolution, the European Catholic Church also became the enemy of the liberal principles once associated with hostile revolutionary energies.

During the late eighteenth and early nineteenth centuries the Catholic Churches in Ireland and the United States evolved in a different direction. The Catholic Church in Ireland, in particular, took a decidedly more favorable view of modern democratic realities and, in fact, developed a liberal tradition on the major questions of the day (i.e., religious liberty, separation of church and state, voluntaryism, and the nature of authority in church and state). This Irish Catholic tradition, transplanted to the United States through Irish immigration, enhanced the already-liberal outlook of many in the American Catholic Church.

When Irish immigrants like John England came to the United States carrying their traditions with them, they were not always accepted, to say the least, as genuine liberals. Not only did their identification of republicanism with Catholicism irritate many of the American Protestant nativists, but their aggressive manner in doing so also disturbed many of their American Catholic neighbors who preferred a low-profile Catholicism in a Protestant country. Protestant nativists perceived the Irish Catholics' advocacy of liberalism as expedient and opportunistic and, therefore, unbelievable. Many native American Catholics found the Irish style foreign to the way the American Catholic minority had dealt with the Protestant majority for centuries. Even though as the majority of the population in Ireland they had suffered from the penal laws imposed upon them by the Protestant minority, the Irish liberals like England had never experienced a minority status in Ireland. Thus, they did not properly appreciate their role as a minority in the United States and, particularly in England's case, failed to understand the persistence of American hostility to Catholicism.

The Irish Catholics' highly visible and aggressive attempts to overcome nativists' enmity created numerous tensions within the Catholic community itself and intensified the hostility between the community and the nativists. Underlying many of the dissensions was the most important ideological and practical issue for the the Catholic Church in the nineteenth century: i.e., the question of the relationship between republicanism and Catholicism. To what extent and by what means should or could the Catholic Church be credibly adapted to the principles and practices of American republicanism without losing its identity? John England's liberal Irish Catholic response to this question was conditioned by his own particular experiences in Ireland and in the United States. In both countries, he advocated religious liberty, separation of church and state, voluntaryism, and, therefore, found no contradiction between Catholic and American positions on these issues. He developed these positions not as a result of his theological training, which was hostile to these positions, but as a consequence of his creative reflections upon the political and religious experiences of the Irish Catholicism of his day. England also called the Catholic Church to accommodate itself to the constitutional forms of government in the modern democratic world. His own attempts to adapt the church to American circumstances were based upon his conciliar and constitutional views of the church which he developed as a result of his theological training in Gallicanism and his filtering of that theology through encounters with British and American constitutionalism. Throughout his ministry in the United States, therefore, England taught that the constitutionalism inherent in Catholicism was consistent with the constitutional basis of American republican government. For England, constitutionalism was the precise meeting point of Catholicism and American republicanism, even though the one was of divine and the other of human origin.

In order to present systematically John England's approach to American Catholicism and republicanism, Section I sketches the political and ecclesiastical reforms in early nineteenth-century Ireland which nurtured England's development. Section II reconstructs the pertinent ideological issues which supported those reforms and which have a particular bearing upon the immigrant's American experiences; it also delineates England's specific ideological positions. Sections III and IV reveal the problems England encountered as an immigrant bishop in the United States, describe the practical procedures he initiated to solve the conflicts, develop the ideological positions which supported his programs, and indicate precisely how American circumstances conditioned his theological perceptions of the church and in which ways he departed from some of his earlier positions in Ireland.

KEY TO ABBREVIATIONS

AAB   Archdiocesan Archives of Baltimore

CMC   *Cork Mercantile Chronicle*

HRS   *Historical Records and Studies*

RACHS   *Records of the American Catholic Histori-
                           cal Society of Philadelphia*

REPERTORY I   [John England], *The Religious Repertory
                           for the Year of Our Lord 1809: Being a
                           Collection of Monthly Publications con-
                           taining a number of Original Essays on
                           Religious Subjects; Lives of Most of the
                           Glorious Apostles, and of other Remark-
                           able Persons. A Variety of Extracts from
                           the most approved religious Authors;
                           interesting Documents; Remarkable
                           Occurrences and Deaths* (Cork: J. Haly
                           Publisher, 1810)

REPERTORY II   [John England], *The Religious Repertory
                           for the Year of Our Lord 1814: Being a
                           Choice Collection of Original Essays, on
                           Various Religious Subjects; Extracts
                           from the Holy Fathers, and other ap-
                           proved authors; Lives of the Principal
                           Saints, and other Distinguished
                           Catholics; Curious and interesting
                           Documents and All Occurrences Re-
                           garding Religion* (Cork: Charles Dillon,
                           1814)

REPERTORY III   [John England], *The Religious Repertory.*
                           No. 19 (January, 1815); No. 20
                           (February, 1815); No. 21 (March, 1815)

USCM   *United States Catholic Miscellany*

WORKS   Ignatius A. Reynolds (ed.), *The Works of
                           the Right Reverend John England* (5
                           vols.; Baltimore: John Murphy & Co.,
                           1849)

SECTION I

irish catholic reform movements: 1800-1820

Irish Catholicism during the early nineteenth century experienced both reform and conflict. Two major reform movements, the one political and the other religious, gradually, but profoundly, transformed Irish Catholicism during the period, molded the minds and attitudes of John England and other Irish Catholics who emigrated to the United States, and influenced the American Irish Catholics who observed those developments from their new homes in America. The political reform campaign increased the political consciousness and effectiveness of the Irish Catholic, and induced a religious reform movement which eventually renewed the structures and life of the Irish Catholic Church. Both of these reforms brought new tensions to the Irish Catholic experience, and strengthened and intensified the old class conflicts of eighteenth-century Irish society among the peasants, the gentry, and the ruling Protestant minority. As a young priest, John England participated actively in both reform movements, became involved in the conflicts, and thus, unknowingly prepared himself for many of his later American experiences.

John England and the influence of Irish Catholicism upon American Catholicism can be understood adequately only within the context of late eighteenth-century Irish experience. The conditions of that period not only gave rise to the political and religious reforms in the early nineteenth century, but also influenced many of the conflicts within American Catholicism during the same period. This section, therefore, outlines briefly the basic characteristics and major events of late eighteenth-century Irish Catholicism before focusing upon the two major reforms.

CHAPTER I

eighteenth-century irish catholicism

Three historical circumstances conditioned Irish Catholicism during the late eighteenth century. First, because of the British penal code against Catholicism, Irish Catholics were deprived of social, economic, and political rights. Second, even though the penal system had systematically disorganized the ecclesiastical structures of Irish Catholicism and had hindered the development of a vibrant religious life, nonetheless it unintentionally planted seeds of strength and vitality in the Catholic community. During the late eighteenth century, the seeds began to develop and reached full maturity in the nineteenth-century immigrant Catholic communities in the United States. Third, because the penal laws were not rigorously enforced during this period and because they were slowly being abrogated, Irish Catholicism was beginning to recover and to revive some of its ecclesiastical life and structures.

When the historian describes eighteenth-century Irish Catholicism, he cannot do so without referring to the devastating effects of the penal laws which have a long and complicated history.[1] They originated in the late seventeenth century, were added to and became most severely executed during the first quarter of the eighteenth century, but, after the middle of the eighteenth century, were rarely enforced with any rigor. After 1788, in particular, they were gradually mitigated and were substantially abrogated in 1829.

The penal system had a number of effects upon Irish Catholicism in the late eighteenth century. By the 1770's, for all practical purposes, the laws had deprived Irish Catholics of most of their political and civil rights, and had almost completely destroyed the Catholic landed class. Thus, the codes effectively eliminated much Catholic political consciousness. Although the laws against Catholic education, worship, bishops and clergy were not always enforced with regularity and severity, nonetheless they seriously restricted the development of ecclesiastical structures and institutions.[2] The Irish Parliament's inability or lack of desire to enforce the laws also produced a deleterious result. As Maureen Wall indicates, "the system adopted by the Government of leaving savage laws on the statute book while conniving at their non-observance brought all law into contempt" (Wall 1961: 69). Even though the Irish Parliament had little effective power to enforce the full rigor of the many detailed laws against Catholics, nonetheless the codes themselves had an almost mythical power and could be periodically invoked as a threat against the Irish Catholic. They were, thus, a constant reminder of the inferior status of Catholicism in the Kingdom. In this way, they served not so much to convert Irish Catholics to Protestantism -- although that did happen among some of the gentry -- as to preserve the political, economic, and social dominance of the British Protestant minority.[3] As a result of these laws, moreover, a permanent barrier was established between things British and Irish -- where Irish Catholicism was seen as the "besieged way of life" and the British Government and Protestantism "an alien force" (McCaffrey 1973: 527; Corish 1968: 57). Contrariwise, throughout the penal period, Catholicism was increasingly identified with Irish culture. Thus, the penal laws drew battle lines which lasted well into the twentieth century between Irish Catholicism and British Protestantism (Mooney 1967: 19).

Ironically, the penal laws also produced benefits for the Irish Catholic Church. As indicated above, the code unintentionally planted seeds of strength in the Irish Catholic community. The statutes created an experience of persecution for both the laity and the clergy, cementing them in a common bond which continued into the twentieth century.[4] The laws also made the Catholic Church a voluntary religious institution. In Ireland, belonging to the Catholic Church was a voluntary experience -- even though the identification of Catholicism with Irish culture may have somewhat lessened the voluntary nature of that experience. Nonetheless, Irish Catholics not only belonged to their church voluntarily (and many times suffered because of their choice), but freely supported their clergy and the church with their meager financial assistance. Unlike many of the major European and

American churches during the penal days, the Irish Catholic Church supported itself while simultaneously paying tithes for the Established Church. This experience of voluntaryism would prove to be a great asset for Irish and American Catholicism in the nineteenth and twentieth centuries.

The penal code, moreover, continually reminded Irish Catholics that Ireland was a Protestant State in which the Anglican Church was established and in which Catholics were denied political and civil rights. Living under such circumstances, Irish Catholics actually experienced a separation of church and state (i.e., the Catholic Church was not a legally-established State church) that no other Christian community which represented a majority of a country's population had ever experienced. Separation meant that the British Government was not directly involved in the internal operation of the Irish Catholic Church; it was, therefore, a free church. This experience of separation was not completely realized in Irish Catholicism, however, until the death of the Stuart Pretender, James III, in 1766. From 1687 until 1766, almost all the bishops appointed to Irish sees were chosen on the nomination of the Stuarts. After 1766, the papacy no longer acknowledged the Stuarts as kings of England and Ireland; thereafter, the Catholic Church enjoyed in Ireland a greater freedom from any state interference in its own internal operations (particularly in the selection of clergy and the determination of ecclesiastical policies) than it did in all other European countries (Wall 1961: 19, 20, 69-70; Giblin 1971: 47, 51-52; M. O'Connell 1971: 18; M. O'Connell 1975: 176-78).

The experience of the penal system, furthermore, encouraged Irish Catholics to perceive the union of church and state as inimical to their own interests. The practical experience of such a union also made them skeptical of traditional beliefs about religious liberty and church-state relations, and gradually induced them to develop liberal principles of religious liberty and separation of church and state. Thus, even though Irish Catholics suffered deprivation because of the penal system, nevertheless they also enjoyed common bonds between the clergy and the laity, voluntaryism, and separation of church and state -- all of which gave them internal resources for overcoming the disabilities they suffered under the penal laws and prepared them for accommodating themselves to American principles and practices.

The gradual and steady organizational revival of the Irish Catholic Church was one of the more remarkable events of the late eighteenth century. The recovery of ecclesiastical structures after the disorganization created by penal legislation during the early eighteenth century, the development of greater Irish Catholic political consciousness and activity, and the beginnings of a liberal Irish Catholic political and religious intellectual tradition were the results of numerous internal and external stimuli. The internal dynamism of the persecuted community, the development of an articulate Irish Protestant political leadership, and the American and French Revolutions contributed significantly to the Catholic recovery. Because of the American and French Revolutions, in particular, the Irish and British Parliaments passed a number of relief bills for Irish Catholics in 1778, 1782, 1792 and 1793. The French Revolution had a further liberating effect upon Irish Catholics in that it created a more favorable image of the Catholic Church in England.[5] Thus, after 1793, Irish Catholics were released from many of the penal codes and admitted to most of the privileges of British society. They could enter many of the professions formerly prohibited, erect their own schools, and vote in Irish elections; but a number of prohibitions remained. Catholics still did not possess political power, could not sit in parliament, nor could they rise to higher positions in the legal or military professions (Lecky 1871: 130). Nonetheless, Catholics were beginning to enjoy a greater degree of emancipation than they had throughout much of the eighteenth century.

Although Irish Catholic leaders were not responsible for passing the relief acts of the late eighteenth century, they did lead political pressure groups which encouraged the relaxation of the penal laws. In 1757, an association of Irish Catholic gentry and merchants drew up an oath of political allegiance to the government in order to persuade the Irish and British Parliaments to grant them some relief from the penal system (See MacCaffrey 1909: II, 102-07). The leadership was politically timid, however. Their effort accomplished almost nothing, but the public appearance of a Catholic association was a first sign of an evolving Catholic political awareness. In the 1770's, a bolder step into the public arena was taken by the Cork priest Father Arthur O'Leary, one of Ireland's seminal thinkers on religious liberty and one of John England's primary intellectual progenitors.[6] According to O'Leary's biographer Thomas England, when O'Leary came to prominence in Cork, the Irish Catholic lacked any discernible political consciousness. The Irish, England noted, "knew little, and cared less, about the distinctions of a king *de jure* and a king *de facto*; of the social compact and the sovereignty of the people they are equally ignorant" (T. England 1822: 30; cf. Lecky 1871: 132). O'Leary awakened the Irish Catholics from their political slumber. He was the first major eighteenth-century Catholic figure to enter the field of public debate and to promote and defend openly the cause of Irish Catholicism. He also published numerous pamphlets on the Catholic views of religious and civil liberty (O'Leary 1781). Even though he did not enter forcibly into any political movement, he did have an effect on Catholic public opinion, particularly in his native city of Cork. More practical political achievements were made by the Catholic Committee, a body of landowners and middle class merchants of a loosely representative character. Formed in 1773, the Committee did much to encourage the oath act of 1774 and the relief act of 1778 (See MacCaffrey 1909: II, 107-15). In 1792 and 1793, moreover, under the leadership of John Keogh, Catholics formed a convention of representatives from various counties of Ireland which prepared numerous petitions to the king and to the Parliament for Catholic emancipation (Lecky 1871: 133; MacCaffrey 1909: II, 115-142). By 1794, through the efforts of Keogh and other Catholic leaders, Catholics "had acquired political consciousness, and some measure of political power, and they were no longer to be ignored" (Beckett 1966: 253).

The days of increased political consciousness and the developing movements toward greater civil and religious liberty were, however, to be shortlived. Signs of the coming despair were first evident in 1795 when William Wentworth Fitzwilliam, Lord Lieutenant of Ireland, was recalled to England. He had been sympathetic to appeals for greater civil and religious freedoms for Irish Catholics. With his removal from office, Irish Catholic hopes for future emancipation bills were lost and, according to Lecky, the leaders' dashed hopes led "inevitably" to the rebellion of 1798 (Lecky 1871: 140, 147). The causes of the rebellion, of course, were far more complex and complicated than suggested here; nevertheless, the rebellion was symbolic of a profoundly depressed spirit within the Catholic community in Ireland.

In 1799, following the rebellion and partly because of it, British politicians in Ireland encouraged Irish Protestant and Catholic leaders to support the union of the Irish and British Parliaments. As a means of persuasion, the politicians promised to give the Catholic clergy state financial support and to emancipate the total Catholic population. In return for these concessions, the politicians asked the bishops to grant the government the right to veto future nominations to the Irish episcopacy. The veto, some parliamentarians argued, would give the government security that the bishops selected would not be hostile to the state. The ten episcopal trustees of Maynooth College accepted the measures and were willing to make the grants. In 1800, however, the Union was accomplished with neither the veto nor Catholic emancipation. Irish Catholics' hopes for full emancipation, therefore, were seriously diminished by the end of the eighteenth century. This discouragement, however, did not last long as the events of the early nineteenth century illustrate.

CHAPTER II

irish political reforms: 1800-1820

From the Union of 1800 to the death of King George III in 1820, Irish Catholic leaders on the national and local levels gradually raised Catholic political consciousness and laid the organizational foundations for the massive, non-violent, democratic emancipation movement of the 1820's. Historians have described these political reforms almost exclusively from the perspective of the national Catholic leadership's role (MacDonagh 1903; Ward 1911-12; Gwynn 1928); they have neglected that history from the viewpoint of local city and county involvement, without which the national movements would have been doomed. The remainder of this chapter, therefore, reveals the invaluable contribution of the local campaigns by focusing upon the political activities in the city and county of Cork. Newly-discovered sources disclose, in particular, John England's participation in and perception of those efforts.[7]

THE UNION TO THE VETO

The national Catholic leadership had become politically apathetic as a result of the Union of 1800 (McDougall 1945: 256-57). They felt that the Union had wrecked their chances for Catholic emancipation. The apathy, however, did not endure for long. After the Union until

Catholic emancipation in 1829, new leaders emerged and gradually, but significantly, transformed the Catholic Church from a politically ineffective body into one sensitive to the realities of public pressure and constitutional government. In 1803 (and almost yearly after that date), Dublin Catholic leaders sent a Catholic emancipation petition to Parliament. In the same year, Parliament discussed the possibility of granting Catholic emancipation and state payment of the Catholic clergy in exchange for the right of the British government to veto the nominations of Irish Catholic bishops. The veto question, as it was called, was raised more seriously in 1808 and from 1812 to 1816. At one period during these years Rome was willing to agree to the veto. The Irish Catholics, however, led by a group of Dublin laymen, rose up and repeatedly rejected both British and Roman interference in what they considered the internal affairs of their own national church. In Dublin and eventually in almost every major city in Ireland, laymen organized Catholic committees or Catholic boards to frame petitions to the Parliament against the veto and for unqualified Catholic emancipation. Daniel O'Connell, John England's friend and "fellow agitator," was the most forceful national leader in the resistance against the veto; his position in the history of the Catholic Church has not yet been duly recognized.[8] Through O'Connell and the various county and city Catholic boards and committees throughout Ireland, the priests and eventually the national body of bishops were influenced to join in the struggle for Irish Catholic independence.

While Dublin was the center of national Irish Catholic political activity during the early nineteenth century, it was not the only city of reform energy. Cork, the second largest city in Ireland, also became a center of renewal during this period. Cork Catholics, however, were slow to become politically active. They were only gradually drawn into the national movement. Catholic participation in local political affairs was limited primarily to the Cork Catholic gentry before 1808. In 1808, however, the political situation began to change. In that year, Henry Grattan presented a Catholic emancipation bill to the British Parliament which contained the veto measures. Daniel O'Connell, James Clinch and a number of Dublin Catholic leaders raised a storm of protest against the bill because of the veto clauses and called upon the national Catholic episcopacy to condemn the bill as opposed to Catholic interests in Ireland. The Catholic bishops met in a national meeting in Dublin in response to the call and resolved that it was "inexpedient to introduce any alteration in the Canonical mode hitherto observed in the nomination to Irish Roman Catholic Bishops" (Quoted in *Repertory*, II, 35). In Cork, although there was little organized opposition to Grattan's 1808 proposal, some Catholics did

raise their voices against the measure. Bishop Francis Moylan of Cork
had participated in the national episcopal statement against the veto[9];
the *Cork Mercantile Chronicle*, a Catholic-owned newspaper, expressed opposition to the veto by publishing the letters of Bishop John
Powers of Waterford against the measure and by printing a few
editorials against it.[10] At this time, John England, like many other
Cork Catholics, was not involved in any Cork resistance. He had just
been ordained on October 2, 1808, at the age of twenty-two. A few
months after his ordination, in May of 1809, he began editing a
religious periodical, *The Religious Repertory*, which revealed no interest in the veto; the magazine was exclusively devoted to the reform
of the religious life of Cork Catholics.[11] By and large, the veto question
produced minimal agitation in Cork until it was again presented to the
Parliament in 1810. On March 17, 1810, in response to these new attempts to secure the veto, a Dominican priest, John Ryan, preached a
hostile sermon in the Cork Cathedral against the English Catholics and
particularly against John Milner, Vicar-Apostolic of England's
Midland District, for supporting the veto measures.[12] Shortly after this
sermon, the *Chronicle*, aggravated by Grattan's 1810 emancipation
proposals, again spoke out in opposition to the veto measure saying that
the veto would give the state excessive political influence over the ecclesiastical affairs of Irish Catholics (*CMC*, May 25, 1810).

While the Cork leaders were opposing the veto, the Dublin leaders
again called upon the bishops to condemn Grattan's bill. The bishops
met in response to the call, reaffirmed their 1808 resolutions, and asserted:

> that it appertains to the order, charge and spiritual
> authority of bishops in the Catholic Church, and is
> inseparable from their mission, to propose, entertain
> and judge, without any lay interference, on points of
> Christian faith and of general discipline
> (*Repertory*. II, 35).

By "lay interference," of course, the bishops were referring to and
criticizing Grattan's Bill and governmental intervention in the internal
discipline of the Catholic Church; they were not protesting the Irish
Catholic laity's opposition to or involvement in the veto measure. They
resolved, furthermore, that it was the "undoubted and exclusive right"
of the Roman Catholic bishops to discuss all matters of doctrine and
discipline. They felt that in taking the episcopal oath of loyalty to the
British government they were offering the government enough security
of their loyalty. They also assured the clergy and laity that they neither
sought nor desired any "earthly considerations" (a reference to state

payment of the clergy) from the government in exchange for general Catholic emancipation; they sought and desired only what the laity "may from a sense of religion and duty, voluntarily afford us" (*Repertory*. II, 40-41).

Although a few individuals in Cork were outspoken in their opposition to the veto, no organized opposition arose until 1811. On September 2, 1811, a number of Cork Catholics gathered to organize themselves into a Catholic Committee for the purposes of petitioning Parliament for their emancipation and uniting their resistance to the veto measure. Daniel O'Connell seems to have been one of the primary forces behind this local movement. He was present at the first meeting of the group, spoke for two hours on the aims of the emancipation movement, and helped the members draw up the first Cork Catholic petition to Parliament in favor of Irish Catholic civil and religious liberties. The *Chronicle* rejoiced that Cork Catholics had finally organized themselves to fight for their own liberty; with some degree of scolding, however, the paper charged that Cork was one of the last counties in Ireland to meet on Catholic emancipation (*CMC*. Sept. 2, 1811; cf. O'Farrell 1973: 154). The meetings during the next few months were entirely conducted by laymen; neither John England nor any other cleric participated at this period. Like the agitation on the national level, the enthusiasm on the local level was initiated and sustained by the laity.

The first meetings seem to have had little direct effect upon the Cork population; only gradually did the emancipation campaign gain any popular support. After January 6, 1812, leading Cork Catholics and a few sympathetic Protestants met at periodic intervals to petition Parliament for Catholic emancipation and to encourage more popular support for their crusade. The meetings, called the "Cork Aggregate Meetings" were convoked and reported through the *Chronicle*. the movement's organ of public opinion. The *Chronicle* frequently prodded the members of the aggregate committee to more active and public participation in the Catholic cause and periodically contrasted their lethargy with the energetic activity of many of the aggregate committees in other counties in Ireland (*CMC*, Aug. 19, Sept. 18, 1811; Jan. 6, Mar. 20, 1812). The paper also constantly expressed gratitude to the "enlightened and liberal Protestant brethren" who sided with the Catholic cause and did so at the risk of incurring the wrath of the state.[13]

POLITICAL CONSCIOUSNESS IN CORK

The one event which awakened the political consciousness of the Cork Catholic leadership and brought Father John England into political prominence was the election to the House of Commons in November of 1812. Christopher Hely Hutchinson had been the incumbent Cork representative in the House of Commons. He had consistently advocated the cause of Catholic emancipation and was vigorously opposed to the various veto proposals brought forth in the House of Commons. In the November Cork elections he was defeated. On December 12, 1812, shortly after the results of the election were made known, John England and a number of Catholic laymen met to form an "Association of Independent Roman Catholic Electors of the City of Cork." The defeat of Hutchinson made them realize that they had to make more strenuous efforts to bring out the Catholic vote. England estimated that the population of Cork at the time was about 100,000, of whom 90,000 were Catholics and not twenty of these were registered to vote (*USCM*, Feb., 1827, p. 238). Because England and other Catholics felt that lack of Catholic freeholder participation in the election had caused Hutchinson's defeat, they began to register the freeholders, the only eligible voters of Irish society. At the Association's first meeting, the participants drew up a series of resolutions which condemned the dissension caused by the election, commended Hutchinson for his past support of the Catholic cause, and established a fund for the promotion of the Catholic cause and the support of their candidates in future elections; they also elected England to be secretary of the association and determined that they would henceforth take a more active role in future elections (*CMC*, Dec. 9, 1812). The defeat of Hutchinson, thus became the occasion for one of the first major steps of the Irish clergy into the arena of Irish politics.[14]

The Cork elections were followed by an event of even more importance in arousing popular Cork Catholic support for unqualified Catholic emancipation. In 1813, Henry Grattan presented another veto emancipation bill in Parliament. This bill caused the greatest Cork Catholic opposition up to that time. England and the *Chronicle*, in particular, forcefully opposed it and tried to gain popular support against the measure (*The Freeholder*, Mar. 9, 1813. Cf. also *CMC*, May 10, 26, 31; June 16, 18, 1813). England, the *Chronicle*, and the Dublin anti-vetoists called upon the national body of bishops to condemn the veto unequivocally at their annual meeting in the summer of 1813. When the bishops met that summer they issued their strongest protest to date. Their statement did not refer to the inexpediency of accepting the veto as had their former ones; it declared that,

it would be impossible for us to assent, without
incurring the guilt of SCHISM, inasmuch as they [state
payment of the clergy and the veto] might, if carried
into effect, invade the spiritual jurisdiction of our
supreme Pastor, and alter an important point of our
discipline, for which alteration his concurrence would,
upon Catholic principles be indispensably necessary
(*Repertory*, II, 42).

The bishops felt forced to speak out on this political issue because they
believed their silence might be interpreted as consent to the
arrangements made in the emancipation bill for the veto and state
payment of the Catholic clergy. These measures, they protested,
"*Never can have our concurrence*"; they were "utterly incompatible
with the discipline of our Church, and with the free exercise of our
Religion" (*Repertory*, II, 43). In these increasingly forceful statements
against the veto, the bishops were expressing the opinions of what had
by 1813 become a major Irish Catholic resistance movement. By the
summer of that year, Cork anti-vetoists were a significant part of that
movement. On July 5, 1813, after the bishops had spoken out against
the veto, the Cork Catholic Committee held a "Grand Dinner" in
honor of the Irish Bishops' opposition to the veto and resolved that they
would accept only unqualified emancipation from Parliament (*CMC*,
July 5, 1813).

A propitious event in the summer of 1813 ultimately increased
England's political influence in the Cork community and made him
one of the most prominent clerical leaders of public opinion in the
province of Munster. At this time, the *Cork Mercantile Chronicle* had
fallen into financial difficulties and was at the point of bankruptcy. In
order to save the paper from complete collapse and to continue its
campaign against the veto, England, Bishop Moylan, and a number of
Catholic clergy and laity purchased one half of the paper. At the
urging of his bishop, England assumed the trusteeship of the paper on
June 15, 1813. Although he wrote frequently for the *Chronicle* before
taking over its proprietorship (*Works*, V, 134), as one of the major
editors he strengthened the anti-vetoist position the paper had
previously taken. From this point onward, the paper's opposition to the
veto was theological as well as political.

Being the trustee for a paper was not without its risks in those days in
Ireland; the paper's fearless advocacy of Catholic rights made it subject
to constant suspicion from the British government and the attorney
general. England was in fact sued at least once for libel during the days
of his trusteeship. The suit is of interest because it revealed much of the

spirit which pervaded the publication, showed some of the principles which guided England in conducting a public press, and demonstrated some of the opposition he had to face in Cork because of his part in the paper.[15]

On April 1, 1816, an article appeared in the *Chronicle* which reported an altercation between a peasant tenant and his landlord. In condemning the landlord for exacting what the *Chronicle* considered excessive and unjust rents and in sympathizing with the poor Irish peasantry who were "driven...to desperation" by such measures, the *Chronicle* did "regret to say, that the mesne landlord is a clergyman" (*CMC*, Aug. 30, 1816). No names were mentioned, but the references in the article to the clergyman landlord were enough to indicate the man's identity; the landlord was the Rev. Mr. Wills Crofts, the editor of *The Southern Reporter*. Even though England did not write the article, he was responsible for it as proprietor of the paper. Crofts brought him to trial for libel after he refused to divulge the sources of his information for the article; England maintained that to do so would be injurious to the future of a free press by destroying its accesses to private information (*CMC*, Aug. 28, 1816). The libel suit charged him with intending to wound the feelings, integrity and humanity of the plaintiff. England lost the case and was fined 1200 pounds for damages. After the trial, he protested that the jury was stacked with Protestant landlords, that he was not tried by his peers, and that no attempt was made even to give "the appearance of equality" in the selection of the jury (*CMC*, Aug 28, 1816). On August 30, 1816, England again protested:

> We are by no means questioning the justice of the proceedings; but we cannot help noticing the public remarks upon the singularity of having a jury, exclusively Protestant, to try this case, in which the Plaintiff and the Defendent were clergymen of different Religions (*CMC*).

In the course of the trial, a number of issues were raised which revealed England's political principles and some of the opposition to those principles in Cork. Besides charging England with libel the attorneys for the plaintiff accused England of:

> dealing out in a public Newspaper his political doses, and with an acrimonious venom, keeping alive an angry political controversy, against the canons and laws -- against the peace and happiness of society, through his public prints -- and in an unprecedented manner sacrificing his functions to the indulgence and malignant violation of his sacred office; whether

with the consent of his higher powers to us is not
known.... Gentlemen, I am a lover of the people,
but I am a lover of order; I love the people under our
blessed constitution; but I would not allow that order
to be disturbed by political incendiaries, who
thro' [sic] political views will malign and impugn
every virtue, and disturb the repose and safety of the
people (*CMC*, Aug. 30, 1816; cf. also Sept. 4, 1816).

England was on trial for more than libel; he was on trial for advocating
the sovereignty of the people, political reforms, support of the
peasants' cause; and for causing general disturbances of the public
order. The charges, although not related to this particular case, seem
to have been true. England repeatedly maintained that the movement
he was advocating was the "cause of a People"; it was not the cause of a
Baronet or a Peer or any other group of persons who held vested interests in Ireland (*CMC*, Oct. 1, 1813). The campaign of an entire people must necessarily, England wrote in the *Chronicle* on August 27,
1814, bring some heat; those who opposed the agitation for unqualified
emancipation "may as well expect to behold an ocean without an occa-
sional ebullition of warm and animated feeling." Against the charge of
being an agitator or revolutionary, England told his *Chronicle* readers
on September 22, 1815, that those who advocated political reforms
were only reminding "our people of their wrongs," or telling them of
their rights; those who told people such things were always "upbraided
as revolutionists" or "calumniated as agitators." England held that
when people "seek any reformation they...immediately met [sic] with
the charge of self interested agitation." He asserted that those who constantly opposed change might also claim that the Catholic religion was
a "source of disunion, and its Divine Founder and his apostles the most
guilty agitators that ever appeared among [men] inasmuch as the
change which they sought to establish, was more extensive in its operation than that proposed by any other person or persons whatsoever."
While England was in Ireland, "change" and "reformation" were not
reprehensible concepts because they were identified with the prosperity and development of the Catholic people. To be sure, the Protestant
landlords on the jury did not overlook the *Chronicle's* former liberalism
and England's general advocacy of the cause of the peasant tenantry
nor did they consider lightly the charges of clerical interference in
political affairs.

England's attorneys answered the charges indirectly by supporting
the freedom of the press and the obligation of newspapers to point out
abuses in landlord-tenant relationships; they held that when the
peasantry was oppressed, a public paper had the responsibility to lean

to the side of the unfortunate peasant "who had no other advocate but a free press." In the present case, the attorneys added, England "was only discharging a duty which the Liberty of the Press imposed upon him, namely, as a Proprietor, to notice the intrenchments upon the rights of society in general terms" (*CMC*, Sept. 2, 1816). Had the *Chronicle* printed the article in much more "general terms" instead of specifying the case so pointedly, however, a libel suit might not have arisen. Under British law at the time, libel could be charged against anyone who defamed a person in print, even if the charges against the person were proven true (Inglis 1952: 4). The libel suit revealed the *Chronicle* as a primary advocate of the principles of freedom and social justice during the height of the veto controversy in the years 1813 to 1817 and throughout England's ministry in Ireland.[6]

Although the *Chronicle* was the foremost agency in Cork for the dissemination of Catholic anti-vetoist opinion, the Cork aggregate meetings were the most prominent instrument for political organization. The meetings were held regularly long before the height of the veto controversy, but they were not fully activated and utilized until the summer of 1813. They were composed of Catholic and Protestant anti-vetoists who met frequently after August 30, 1813, until emancipation was achieved in 1829. During the veto years, England seems to have been the only clergyman who participated actively in the meetings. He was recognized as one of the leading voices at the meetings and was usually greeted with unanimous backing when he made specific proposals for resolutions to be sent to Parliament. When hostility broke out in the Cork Catholic Committee after the 1815 Cork elections, Daniel O'Connell suggested that the group appoint England to help solve the difficulties and to mend its wounds (*CMC*, Sept. 1, 1815). O'Connell was frequently present at these Cork meetings. He and England occasionally spoke at great length in outlining the principles upon which the movement was based. On September 5, 1813, for example, at a dinner meeting held to gather more popular support for the emancipation measures, O'Connell spoke for two hours on the nature of religious and civil liberty and on the necessity of keeping the temporal and spiritual areas of a man's life completely independent of one another. At the same meeting, England defended the rights of a clergyman to participate in political agitation because the political issues involved the freedom of the Irish Church. He asserted that as a clergyman, he did not exercise an excessive influence over the body politic. He claimed that he was simply a freeholder who had a political right to vote and to influence others by persuasion in the direction he deemed correct (*CMC*, Sept. 6, 1813).

During the various meetings held from 1813 to 1820, England ex-

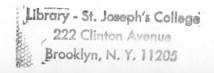

perienced the processes of democratic politics and witnessed the necessity and force of articulated public opinion. Through participation in various discussions and decisions, and in the formation of numerous resolutions for Parliament, he also learned to value democratic methods. All questions, he said once, should be settled by discussion. Once discussions were concluded, the will of the majority should prevail. "The only way to preserve peace and unanimity amongst us," he noted, "is for all persons to support the desire of the majority; even though you should decide against me, I shall acquiesce in your determination" (CMC, Sept. 5, 1814). He did not believe, however, that the individual should simply be a slave to the will of the group; he felt that individuals and minorities had a right to stand alone if their consciences could not accept the majority will.[17]

England's increasingly active role in the anti-veto movement was manifested most clearly in his *Religious Repertory* for the years 1814 and 1815. In those years, he transformed the direction of the periodical. He no longer stressed exclusively the passive nature of Christianity and the need for personal spiritual reform, as he had in the years 1809 and 1810; he was now emphasizing the active role of resistance. For him, opposition to the veto was a religious duty that was necessary to protect the liberty of the church from the political interference of the British government.

ROME AND THE VETO

In the first months of the year 1814, the Cork Aggregate members felt secure that the veto would not be granted and that they could proceed to petition Parliament for unqualified emancipation. On May 9, 1814, however they learned that a papal official of Propaganda, Monsignor John Baptist Quarantotti, had granted the English Catholics a rescript giving them permission to accept the veto measures attached to the Catholic Emancipation Bill. On February 16, 1814, Monsignor Quarantotti had written the Vicar Apostolic of London, William Poynter, indicating that Rome could accept the securities in exchange for Catholic emancipation (Letter found in *Repertory*, II, 48-52). This letter, called the Quarantotti rescript, raised a public furor after it was published in the Irish papers. An immediate burst of energy activated the resistance of Catholics in Cork. England called the rescript "an abominable anti-Irish Document," charged the Monsignor and the English vetoists with "convicted criminality" (CMC, May 9, 1814), and called upon Catholic lay groups, clergy conferences and the national body of bishops to oppose the rescript absolutely as an un-warranted interference of an eighty-one-year-old Vatican bureaucrat in the internal affairs of the Irish Church (*Repertory*, II, 52). On May 18, the Cork Catholic Board drew up resolutions, John England called the Cork clergy together, Bishop William Coppinger of Cloyne and Ross convoked his clergy, and clergy and laity gathered together in almost every city in Ireland to denounce the rescript.[18]

The national body of bishops responded to this general outcry on May 27, 1814, by condemning the Quarantotti proposal. They rejected the rescript by simply reaffirming their previous position (*CMC*, May 30, 1814). In their past resolutions on the veto, the bishops had not com-pletely denied the right of Rome to make arrangements with the English government relative to the nomination of Irish bishops; they had said simply that while the pope was imprisoned no changes in church discipline could be considered. In their 1810 pastoral to the clergy and laity of Ireland, for example, the bishops had indicated that they would not accept any rescripts from Rome as genuine until the pope was restored to freedom (*Repertory*, II, 38). In the historical con-text of May 1814, therefore, they believed that a papal brief could not possibly be authentic.

The May 27, 1814 episcopal resolution against the rescript was not as forceful as some of the anti-vetoists wanted. They accepted the statement, however, as a temporary measure against Roman inter-ference. On June 6, in response to the episcopal position, the Cork Catholics gathered together for a dinner (one of many held during these years) to celebrate the universal Irish opposition to the rescript and to congratulate their bishops who had united with them and represented their feelings to Pope Pius VII who had just been released from his captivity (*CMC*, June 6, 1814). On August 26, O'Connell was present at another Cork aggregate meeting where numerous self-congratulatory speeches were given and where a determination was made to continue opposition to the veto until it was no longer an issue either for the British government or for the papal court (*CMC*, Aug. 26, 31, 1814). Frequent similar meetings were held from September through December of that year.

During the first three months of 1815, the Cork Catholics continued their opposition to Roman interference. In May of that year, they learned that another Roman official had attempted to give papal sanc-tion to the Quarantotti rescript. On April 26, 1815, Lawrence Cardinal Litta, the prefect of the Congregation Propaganda Fide, wrote to Poynter essentially confirming the message of the Quarantotti rescript and indicating that Pope Pius VII, now freed from his long imprison-ment, was ready "to accede to and permit" the veto if emancipation

could thereby be achieved. Litta also stated that after the Emancipation Act was passed, the pope would write a brief to the bishops and
Catholics of Great Britain to exhort them to adhere with loyalty to
their government and to the king who had helped to secure the pope's
release (Litta letter in Brenan 1864: 680-82). In response to the Litta
letter, the anti-vetoist press protested unanimously against Roman interference. On August 23, 1815, the bishops confirmed the public dissent by issuing their strongest resolutions to date on the veto; for them,
the veto "must essentially injure, and may eventually subvert, the
Roman Catholic religion in this country." They declared themselves
"unequivocally" opposed to the interference of the British government
in the discipline of the Irish church. After words of veneration for the
pope they unhesitatingly declared that,

> we do not conceive that our apprehensions for the safety
> of the Roman Catholic Church in Ireland can or ought to
> be removed by any determination of his Holiness, adopted,
> or intended to be adopted, not only without our concur-
> rence, but in direct opposition to our repeated resolu-
> tions (Resolutions in *CMC*, Aug. 22, 1817; and J. O'Connell
> 1860: II, 17).

In August of 1815, while the bishops were writing their letter to the
pope, the Dublin laity were preparing to send the Franciscan priest
Richard Hayes to the Vatican to represent the Irish laity's resistance to
British and Roman interference in their local church affairs. Hayes
subsequently spent two years in Rome attempting to thwart any efforts
to have the veto passed through the Roman courts (Brenan 1864:
608f.). On September 8, 1815, the Dublin laity again met and sent to
the pope a remonstrance, written by Daniel O'Connell, expressing
their unanimous sentiments against the veto (J. O'Connell 1860: II, 28-
34).

The pope neither accepted Hayes nor responded to the Dublin lay
remonstrance; moreover, he did not answer the Irish bishops'
statement until February 1, 1816, when he wrote the Irish bishops to
justify his position on the right of the church to establish concordats
with governments for the benefit of religion. The pope felt that the
Irish bishops had over-reacted in declaring that the veto would destroy
religion in Ireland. He confirmed Cardinal Litta's letter to Bishop
Poynter by saying:

> That those whose province it is may present to the King's
> Ministers the list of the Candidates, in order that if
> there be amongst them the name of any person displeasing
> to, or suspected by the Government, such name may be

> immediately pointed out and erased, still, however, so
> that a sufficient number may remain from which his Holi-
> ness may freely choose whom, in the Lord, he may judge
> more fit for presiding over the vacant Sees.[19]

The basis for such an agreement, the pontiff pointed out, could be
found in many concordats made between his predecessors and Catholic
as well as Protestant governments. He declared that only bishops
favorable to state governments should be appointed to dioceses. In
support of this view the pope then quoted from St. Leo: "that none be
ordained Bishops without the consent and postulation of the flock, lest
no unwelcome intruder incur its contempt or hatred." This principle
applied, he noted, not only to the flock, but,

> must rightfully be extended to Princes, the necessary
> circumstances concurring, and even to those who are
> not in communion with us, who from the nature of their
> power in temporal affairs, have so easily the means of
> preventing a Bishop, who may be the object of their
> dislike or suspicion, from the care of the flock committed
> to his charge.

The pope then continued to argue against the Irish fears that the
government would eliminate the names of all those who would not be
subservient to the Throne. He pointed to the past performance of the
British government; it had helped to secure his own release and in the
recent past it had increased the freedom of Irish Catholics. He noted,
moreover, that even before the Protestant Reformation, bishops were
chosen by the pope "upon the supplication of the King." He hoped, furthermore, he was "speeding up emancipation" by permitting the veto.
In support of the changes he desired in Irish ecclesiastical discipline,
the pope quoted St. Leo again:

> As there are certain things which can on no account be
> altered, so are there many which, from a due consider-
> ation of times, or from the necessity of things it may be
> right to modify.

Pope Innocent III had also recognized this principle when he advocated a reform in discipline in the following manner:

> It is not to be considered blameable if, in the
> consequence of a change of times, a change of human laws
> also be effected, especially when an *urgent necessity [sic]*.
> or an evident utility calls for such a change.

The pope, therefore, supported a revision of present discipline that he believed would promote the progress of religion in Great Britain. His letter, however, did not change the attitudes of the majority of those involved in the emancipation movement; they still resisted all attempts to pass the veto measures.

RENEWED POLITICAL AGITATION

By September of 1816, John England noticed that enthusiasm for the cause of Catholic emancipation was beginning to wane. He remarked in one of the aggregate meetings that "there is now the appearance of a general apathy throughout the land" (CMC, Sept. 13, 1816; cf. also Orthodox Journal, IV September, 1816, 358-67). By that time the veto opposition was no longer necessary because Rome had not pressed the issue; veto measures were no longer attached to the Catholic emancipation bills, and every emancipation bill had been rejected by the Parliament. Enthusiastic popular support for future emancipation petitions, therefore, gradually decreased. England, however, tried to overcome the inertia and to revive the spirit of the anti-veto resistance by calling upon each county to press Parliament persistently for unqualified emancipation. He urged especially the Cork Aggregate meetings to continue their agittaion even though they were the only county in the land to do so (CMC, July 21, 1817).

In July of 1817, when it was revealed that Father Richard Hayes had been "abused" by the pope, Cardinal Ercole Consalvi (the papal secretary of state), and the Dublin lay Catholics, political fervor was rekindled in Cork. Hayes had evidently insulted the pope and some of the members of Cardinal Consalvi's staff during his fight for the Irish cause in Rome. The pope, therefore, ordered him to be removed from Italy. He was deported to the Italian borders, and then he returned to Ireland. He had spent two years in Rome without receiving a papal hearing for the Irish laity's case. When he returned to Dublin, the Dublin lay Catholic Board voted not to pay for his two-year mission because of his "improprieties" in Rome. When the Cork Catholics heard these details, they convoked aggregate meetings on July 14 and 21 to support Hayes and to decry his unjust treatment in Rome. Roman intrigue, they claimed, had insulted Ireland by ignoring Hayes (CMC, July 14, 21, 1817). By this time, England had already been made pastor of Bandon, thirty miles south and west of Cork, but that did not take him out of Cork political activities. On February 27, 1818, he wrote a letter to the

editor of the *Chronicle* in support of Hayes and indicated that he had
collected funds from the Bandon "friends of civil and religious liberty"
to defray the expenses of Hayes' two-year mission in Rome. According
to O'Connell, England was the first person in Ireland to take such a
concrete step in raising money to assist Hayes (*Dublin Evening Post,*
April 25, 1818). Others throughout Ireland followed his example. Cork
Catholics, for instance, organized a dinner in honor of Hayes to raise
capital for his cause. Those in Cork who did not support Hayes'
mission, however, were extremely critical of Catholic attempts to aid
him. "We cannot conclude without observing," one editor remarked,
"that it appears somewhat inconsiderate at such a moment as the
present, to be advertising public feasts in the Newspapers while the
streets are crowded with hundreds of starving Poor."[20] So much
Catholic energy and financial aid were poured into the political reform
movements in Cork that probably little was left for other social reform
movements.

Interest in the Hayes affair again awakened Catholics in Cork to active political participation; the issue also reminded them of their own
political power and prepared them for the 1818 elections to the House
of Commons. The campaign of that year caused another great stir in
Cork. England became most actively involved in the affair.[21] Since the
elections of 1812, he had been encouraging the forty-shilling
freeholders to register to vote in the city and county elections. According to some of his contemporaries, he was one of the first men in
Ireland to realize the potential power of the forty-shilling
freeholders.[22] During the campaign of 1818, Christopher Hely Hutchinson, who was again running for office, chose the "political priest"
as one of his campaign managers. Consequently, England travelled
throughout the city frequently stumping for Hutchinson.[23] He felt that
he was a pioneer in these political activities, but he also believed that
his participation in favor of Hutchinson was necessary because Irish
politics was intimately connected with the affairs of the Irish Catholic
Church.[24] Hutchinson favored unqualified Catholic emancipation and
was in England's view, therefore, incorruptible. England's involvement in Hutchinson's campaign brought out the Catholic vote
and, of course, victory for Hutchinson. After the election, Hutchinson
attributed much of the success of his campaign to England's participation and friendship (*Southern Reporter*, July 14, 1818). Later, in
1825, when Daniel O'Connell testified before a committee of the House
of Lords, he was asked if he knew of certain instances in which the
Catholic clergy had "interfered" in county and city elections in
Ireland. After denying that he knew anything of the questioners'
examples of interference, he acknowledged that he knew of John

England's involvement in the Cork elections: "It was principally managed by one of the cleverest, and I think one of the worthiest, men I ever knew" (*Evidence* 1825: 196).

The excitement created by the campaign, election, and the political victory of 1818 set the stage for renewed efforts to petition Parliament for Catholic claims. In the months of January and February of 1819, England's "indefatigable exertions" brought about a union of Catholics and some Protestants in the Protestant city of Bandon in favor of petitioning Parliament for unqualified civil rights (*Cork Advertiser*, Feb. 13, 1819. Cf. also *Southern Reporter*, March 27, 1819). Many Protestants, however, signed petitions against the Catholic resolutions and asked Parliament not to grant Catholic emancipation on the grounds that such a measure would ultimately injure the British Constitution.[25] England was a source of irritation to a number of these Protestants, especially when he sent declarations in favor of Catholic freedoms from Protestant Bandon to Parliament, the Lord Lieutenant of Ireland, and Lord Donoughmore (*Southern Reporter*, May 6, 1819).

The political reform movements among the Catholics of Cork from 1800 to 1820, under the leadership of Catholic lawyers and merchants with the support of John England, like the national campaigns, did not achieve their intended effect -- the passing of an unqualified Catholic emancipation bill in the British Parliament. The 1819 petitions, the last before England left for the United States, were defeated in Parliament by only two votes. Although the agitations did not achieve their intended purposes, they did not fail entirely as movements of political reform. From the years 1812 to 1820, the campaigns in Cork raised the political consciousness of the freeholders, brought the Catholic episcopacy into prominence in Ireland, established a political base for future activity, enrolled the first of the native Irish clergy in the struggle, deepened the political bond among Catholics and propelled the Catholic body politic into the forefront of political reform in Ireland and Great Britain. England played a major role in producing these effects in Cork. His participation brought him into contact with some of the leading political thinkers and agitators of the day, acquanted him with the techniques of democratic politics, helped him to perceive the church as a force within a democratic climate, gave him an experience of the nature and diversity of the various roles within church and society, and induced him to pursue with greater zeal the ecclesiastical reforms of the period.

CHAPTER III

---

church reforms in Ireland: 1800-1820

The increasing civil freedoms, deepening political consciousness, and active Catholic leadership in the anti-veto movements created an atmosphere in late eighteenth and early nineteenth-century Ireland which made possible a greater degree of ecclesiastical reformation than hitherto had been feasible. Some ecclesiastical reforms were directly influenced by the political atmosphere; others were indirectly affected by them; and still others were independent of the political circumstances. During England's days in Ireland (1786-1820), there were at least three major ecclesiastical reform efforts: (1) to create greater internal unity and a more structured external organization within the Irish Church; (2) to renew the general religious and moral life of the people; (3) to establish educational programs. These reforms had not completely matured nor were they universally or systematically organized at this period, but here and there they were beginning to have an effect upon Irish ecclesiastical life.

THE NEED FOR REFORM

Because of the effects of the penal system upon the organization and life of Irish Catholicism, reforms were essential. The penal laws, particularly during the late seventeenth and early eighteenth centuries, had had a devastatingly disruptive effect upon the episcopal structure of the Irish Church. Bishops and regular clergy were banished from Ireland; many bishops, therefore, governed their dioceses as absentee rulers for much of the first quarter of the eighteenth century. Because of the absentee episcopacy during that time, clergy and laity gained an almost absolute authority regarding their congregational life (Wall 1961: 15, 38, 41; Brady and Corish 1972: 27-29). Although all the bishops had returned to Ireland by the middle of the eighteenth century and even though they were gradually restoring order to their dioceses, still the effects of the earlier penal days lingered on in Ireland throughout the late eighteenth and early nineteenth centuries. During the late eighteenth century, in particular, the bishops had little effective power or authority within the national or local church; they had not met in national or provincial gatherings during the eighteenth century; they had almost no unity and very few uniform laws or regulations to govern the national church. In their own dioceses, moreover, they had neither much power nor authority even though some of them held diocesan synods or regular clerical conventions. In some congregations, the parish priests were almost the sole ecclesiastical leaders of the Irish Church; their authority and ministry seem to have been independent of episcopal control. Accordingly, the local parish congregations were almost the only ecclesiastical unit with much real power. Thus, much of Irish Catholicism throughout the period developed along congregational lines. Even though episcopal structure was somewhat visible, nevertheless congregationalism was the primary mode of ecclesiastical life for many Irish Catholics.

The nature of Irish Catholic society also added to disunity and disorganization within the church. Three kinds of Catholicism, it seems, divided the church: that of the aristocracy, the rising middle class, and the peasantry. The Catholicism of the aristocracy was composed of many of the bishops, priests and gentry who were almost completely submissive to the constituted ecclesiastical and governmental authorities. The Catholicism of the rising middle class was comprised of a few bishops, some of the Irish priests and many of the lawyers and merchants who were politically sensitive and democratically oriented. The Catholicism of the Irish peasantry was made up of a few sympathetic Irish clergy, and the mass of the Irish peasantry who were uneducated, unsophisticated, politically unaware, poor, superstitious, and at times rebellious. These diverse experiences of Catholicism created tensions and conflicts within the Irish church.[26]

The local parish structure and the religious, moral and educational life of the parish unit, in particular, needed to be reformed.[27] As already noted, the parish unit in nineteenth-century Irish Catholicism was an independent ecclesiastical unit. In some parishes, the sense of independence sometimes created friction and factions between some of the parishioners and their priests, and between some of the priests and their bishops. Conflicts apparently arose, for example, when some of the laity preferred one particular priest to the episcopally-appointed pastor; priests who were favored by the people seem to have appealed to the "right of patronage" to support their position as legitimate pastors. At times, the bishops of a particular province found it necessary to condemn this situation and to suspend priests who were the cause of such frictions or who interfered with the episcopal appointment of the pastor.[28]

Because of the separation or independence of the parish unit from the effective control and supervision of the local bishop, the clergy and laity developed some ecclesiastical customs and practices which were either immoral or superstitious. The people and the bishops charged some of the clergy with at least four major clerical crimes: drunkenness (*Acta et Decreta*, III, 766), concubinage (*Acta et Decreta*, III, 765), greed, and authoritarianism. The peasantry, in particular, frequently complained that priests were infected with the vice of greed.[29] Rather than relying upon the free-will offerings of the laity for their material sustenance, some priests frequently charged excessive fees for clerical services (i.e., baptisms, marriages, funerals, visits to the sick, etc.).[30] The peasantry were even more disturbed by some of the priests' authoritarianism and their alignment with the despotic landlords and the governmental officials who oppressed the peasantry by their laws and customs (R.E. Burns 1962: 152).

Because of some of these clerical abuses, particularly those of greed and authoritarianism, and because of a general dissatisfaction with their state in Irish society, the poor peasantry at times rose up in rebellion as the only recourse against the injustices of their parish clergy and their landlords. The peasants periodically and openly opposed their priests, robbed them,[31] and even murdered them.[32]

In addition to the clerical vices and peasant uprisings there were many abuses in the people's religious observances and popular piety. Many Irish Catholics apparently failed to attend Mass on Sundays and holy days of obligation (*Acta et Decreta*, III, 767); they also developed a number of immoral and superstitious practices connected with wakes and funerals. Some, for example, were in the habit of using whiskey and other strong liquors on these occasions; they also created mock imitations of the rites of the church and used loud, "unchristian" and "unnatural screams" during the funerals (*Statuta* 1813: 105-108; Brady and Corish 1972: 79-80). Other Irish Catholics sometimes developed superstitious forms of popular piety which catered to the social or folk needs of some of the Irish peasantry. One example of such piety flourished in the parish of St. John the Baptist in Gougan Barra, County Cork. The parish held an annual devotion to their patron saint, John the Baptist. Irish Catholics made pilgrimages to the parish from throughout the entire province of Munster to join in the yearly September celebrations. The festival was an occasion for "drunkenness, debauchery and rioting," according to the Bishop of Cork; it disturbed the peace and brought religion "into disrepute." In addition to the public disorder caused by the celebration, the pilgrims indulged in numerous superstitious practices; they drank and bathed in the waters of the parish's "miraculous" well in expectation of corporeal and supernatural cures, or they dipped their cattle into the well hoping for similar benefits for their livestock. Because of these practices, the feast of the patron saint was suppressed on June 12, 1817, the parish was interdicted and the pilgrims who went to Gougan Barra were excommunicated by order of the Bishop of Cork who administered the sentence in union with John England and a conference of his priests.[33]

Superstitious practices, like those of Gougan Barra, reveal, among other things, the poor state of religious instruction at the time. The penal laws had proscribed Catholic education for the clergy and laity for three centuries. Even after the educational relief acts of 1782, when Catholics were allowed some participation in creating their own schools, they had neither the financial capacity nor the personnel to respond to the extensive need of educating the poor Irish Catholic peasantry. Instructional facilities and programs were still another vital need in the reform of Irish Catholicism.

REFORM OF THE EPISCOPACY

The Irish bishops developed three reform programs corresponding to the needs; they reorganized the national and local episcopacy, revised the ecclesiastical laws regarding the religious and moral life of the priests and people, and revitalized educational programs for the clergy and people. The reorganization of the episcopacy was the most important single development which brought about an eventual reform program within the Irish church. Because of the political pressures, particularly the resistance to the veto, the bishops had to meet annually from 1808 to 1820 to respond to the lay demands for episcopal opposition to the veto. These meetings took place not only on the national, but also on the provincial levels; some bishops also assembled periodically with the priests of their dioceses. The frequent gatherings increased the visibility and strengthened the power of the episcopacy; they also put the bishops in a position in Irish society they had not had before the veto question. Because the bishops backed the opposition to the veto, they gained the support of their clergy and many of their politically-sensitive, middle-class laity. Thus, the political forces laid the foundation for the religious reform measures which resulted from a number of these episcopal meetings.

The political movements were also directly responsible for the attempts to reform the process of nominating bishops to vacant sees in Ireland. The organizational reform of the Irish church demanded a strong, well-informed, and Irish episcopacy. The establishment, therefore, of an effective means of "electing" the best priests for the episcopacy was essential.[34] The veto question, in particular, had raised the question of the proper mode of nominating bishops for vacant sees in Ireland. Because no established or uniform system for such elections existed and because the ecclesiastical law in Ireland was not clarified at the time, the Irish Catholic clergy and laity proposed various modes of electing bishops. The anti-vetoists, in particular, preferred a form of the domestic nomination. They disagreed among themselves, however, on the precise form the nomination should take.

The French theologian Louis Delahogue, who taught at Maynooth and who had been called upon to give his opinion on the doctrinal and disciplinary issues involved in the veto question, believed that by law only the Metropolitan and the provincial bishops were the "electeurs necessaires."[35] Only they were legally qualified to decide upon the appointment of bishops; on certain occasions they not only could but ought to decide by themselves without consulting the people (Delahogue 1797: 187). In support of his position, he argued that even St. Cyprian attacked the election of Novatian on the grounds that it was "contrary to the laws of the church" and to those of the gospel (Ibid., 189). The consent of the people, he declared, was neither "necessary" nor "essential" because the church had used many ways of nominating bishops in the past without such approval (Ibid., 193). The involvement of secular princes in the nomination of bishops, moreover, was for him an historical abuse (Ibid., 192). Delahogue's position that laymen and lay governments should not have a voice in the selection of bishops supported the anti-vetoist claims. His argument that the

Metropolitan and provincial bishops should elect bishops to vacant sees, however, was rejected by many of the anti-vetoists, especially John England.

Although most suggestions advanced for domestic nomination did not include the lay voice, neither did they rely solely upon the Metropolitan and provincial bishops, as did Delahogue's proposals. Most of the plans limited the rights of the Metropolitan and his suffragans and stressed the rights of parish priests and canons (Brenan 1864: 613-15). John England favored some form of domestic nomination which would restore the rights of election to the priests. The discussion of the proper mode of nominating a bishop to a vacant see had begun in Cork in May of 1814, during the peak of the veto controversy. During that month, the clergy of the diocese of Cloyne and Ross and their bishop, William Coppinger, requested the national body of bishops to institute a "defined and authentic organ" of recommending candidates for vacant sees. The clergy drew up a resolution which suggested that all future candidates be natives and residents of the Kingdom of Great Britain, and that this could be "effectually attained by the revival of canonical elections, by the chapter or clergy of the diocese" (CMC, May 20, 1814; cf. also CMC, Aug. 29, 1817). In June of the same year England approved this general proposal (CMC, June 8, 1814; cf. also CMC, Sept. 17, 1817). While the Cloyne clergy and England were calling for such reforms, seven new bishops were appointed to Irish sees; six of them had been selected, according to England, "in the only [way] in which they should, by the canon law, be selected, by the Parish priests, collected in chapter with the Dean at their head" (Repertory, II, 431). The one who had not been elected in this way was the Co-adjutor of Cashel who had been nominated solely by the Archbishop of Cashel. England called upon the clergy to "defeat" this "oppressive system of Nepotism and Favoritism, which has been occasionally resorted to," in Irish nominations. He rejected it because "we never can approve of any system of appointment, which pointedly disregards the will of those who must naturally be most affected by the will of such Governor."[36] The objection was based upon ancient practices found in the Acts of the Apostles, church councils, and the writings of numerous church Fathers.[37]

On August 13, 1817, while he was pastor of Bandon and dean of the district of Bandon, England gathered the priests of the area together in order to petition the national episcopacy on a number of issues, including the proper mode of nominating the bishop. The clergy drew up a resolution which requested the bishops to establish that mode of domestic nomination "which will give to the clergy of the Second Order, that influence in the appointment of their Prelates which is so congenial to the spirit of the Church" (*CMC*, Aug. 18, 1817).

When Bishop Moylan died in February of 1815, the parish priests of Cork gathered to elect as Vicar Capitular, John Murphy. Since there was no chapter in the diocese, England declared, the right of appointment"devolved to Parish Priests, in virtue of a Bull of Benedict XIV" (*Repertory*, III, 80). The entire election process was printed in the *Chronicle* as an example of what should be done throughout Ireland, wherever no chapter and dean existed (*CMC*, Feb. 15; 1815).

England felt that election by the dean and chapter was the proper mode of nominating bishops. In many dioceses in Ireland, however, there were no chapters. He proposed, therefore, that they be re-established. He agreed with the suggestions of a certain "Patricius" who wrote a number of articles for the *Chronicle* on the nature and purpose of cathedral chapters.[38] Patricius' arguments in favor of domestic nomination and the re-establishment of chapters were based upon the ancient church's customs of domestic nomination by clergy and people. Patricius quoted Cyprian's fifty-second epistle to show that historically the Church practiced elections of the bishops. Cyprian wrote:

> Cornelius was appointed Bishop by the voice of the clergy,
> by the suffrage of the laity, and the College of the ancient
> Presbyters (Quoted in *CMC*, Nov. 27, 1816).

Another priest, James Filan, wrote in the *Chronicle* that "right reason and the laws of civilized society proclaim, that subjects have an inalienable right to have some influence in the appointment of their superiors" (*CMC*, Aug. 6, 1817). According to Patricius, the clergy and laity lost their right to elect their bishops only when temporal powers interfered with the church. (*CMC*, Nov. 29, 1816).

Patricius' arguments in favor of the re-establishment of cathedral chapters also revealed a profound concern among some of the Irish clergy for the promotion of their own canonical rights and powers within the church and a desire to define and limit the rights and powers of a bishop within a diocese. According to Patricius, the re-establishment of the chapter would set rational limits to the "exercise of despotic authority," give the clergy an influence in diocesan decisions, and limit the bishop in the exercise of legislative powers on the temporal affairs of the diocese by requiring him to seek the advice and consent of his chapter in many cases.[39] Seen from another point of view, the chapter would increase the bishop's effectiveness by giving more

responsibility to the priests and by calling upon their talents and interests to aid the general welfare of the diocese and thus free him from
much trouble and anxiety in governing (*CMC*, Dec. 4, 1816).

Many of the bishops were not opposed to the clerical suggestions on
domestic nominations and the re-establishment of chapters; some, in
fact, made similar ones themselves.[40] Others convoked clergy conferences to solicit the priests' opinions on the subject.[41] Bishop James
Doyle of Kildare and Leighlin[42] preferred a domestic nomination of the
following type: the clergy of the vacant diocese should nominate to the
vacant see with the concurrence of the metropolitan and suffragan
bishops of the province; after the three names were chosen, they were
to be sent to the pope for final approval and canonical institution
(*Evidence* 1825: 323-25). Doyle's suggestions for revisions in the mode
of nomination, like other Irish proposals during the early nineteenth
century, did not effect any practical reforms until 1829. These plans,
however, did advocate a more collegial approach to problem-solving
and decision-making within the church. They also recognized the need
for a strong, priestly-elected episcopacy for the renewal of the church.

MORAL AND RELIGIOUS REFORMS

The veto question and the discussions on domestic nomination had
projected the bishop into a position of prominence in Ireland. Some of
the Irish bishops took advantage of their newly-won status by beginning to organize their local provincial and diocesan synods to enact
laws and programs for the internal reform of their churches. How
regularly the four Irish Catholic provinces met in episcopal synods is
difficult to determine. The province of Cashel, however, apparently
gathered "quinquennially" after 1808 to discuss the spiritual condition
of the various dioceses of the province and to enact laws for the reform
of the churches.[43] The provincial bishops of Cashel held their first
council since the Protestant Reformation in Limerick on June 17, 1808,
to enact much-needed religious reforms for the province.[44] Following
the example of the Fathers of the provincial synod of Cologne (1549),
the bishops called synods the "nerves of the body of the church."[45] The
bishops of Cashel attempted to reform their churches in two ways.
First, they enacted several laws against the religious abuses of the day,
applying appropriate censures and penalties for violations of those laws
(*Statuta* 1813: 105-08; 123). Secondly, they prepared a series of
pastoral instructions on the elementary teachings of Christianity.

These Christian lessons were to be read from the pulpit on Sundays and other days of religious obligation (*Ibid.*, 134-51; 152-69; 170-85). Thus, through legislation and Christian education, the bishops hoped to revitalize the church.

Before the provincial bishops initiated moral and educational reform measures through conciliar legislation, other forces had been already at work to accomplish local religious reforms. Some bishops, independent of provincial councils, met with their priests in diocesan synods to enact laws and regulations for the diocesan church (Larkin 1962: 298). Other bishops used different means to bring about renewal in their churches. The Bishop of Cork, for example, had encouraged the development of the Presentation Order of Sisters in order to bring about much-needed changes in the religious and social life of the members of his diocese. Throughout the late eighteenth century, the Presentations were beginning to transform the educational and moral life of the young of the city of Cork. These Cork activities preceded the provincial councils and the political reforms of the early nineteenth century.[46]

From the beginning of his priestly ministry in Cork on October 2, 1808, until his ordination to the episcopacy in September, 1820, John England worked with various groups in the city of Cork to reform the prison system, to promote social welfare for the poor of the city, and to provide the people of Cork with a popular religious literature.[47] His most significant contribution to the religious reform movement in Cork seems to have been his production of a number of religious books and periodicals. His first major literary effort in this area, as already noted, was the publication of a religious periodical in May, 1809. *The Religious Repertory*, was intended to be a literary agent of reform for the "lower orders of society."[48] England purposed to reform the Christian moral life through the dissemination of basic religious knowledge on the church and morality. To fulfill this intention, he wrote a number of short and simple essays on revelation, the meaning of the sacraments, authority in religion, and prayer. He also wrote short summaries of the lives of some of the saints and re-printed excerpts from the Church Fathers and various contemporary Catholic writers.[49]

The *Repertory* was like Chateaubriand's *Beauties of Christianity*, excerpts of which were periodically published in the magazine (*Repertory*, I, 42; II, 118f; III, 20), in that it was an apologetic for the authority of revealed religion (i.e., the Catholic Church). It intended to show "the necessity and the value of revealed religion" by presenting historical sketches of religion's good effects on mankind; it compared these beneficial results to the "state of degradation existing in those quarters of the world where Christianity is unknown" and it contrasted the salutary consequences of religion with the evil effects of preferring the dictates of one's own reason and one's own "fancies, to the authority of religion as revealed and established by our Redeemer" (*Repertory*, I, 1). During the early years of the publication, England emphasized the passive virtues of Christianity. He called upon the Irish servants and all those under the supervision of constituted authorities to follow the primary Christian virtues of respect and obedience; he encouraged every Christian to submit willingly to the difficulties of his state in life (*Ibid.*, 28f.) and to accept the mortification of his neighbor's "disagreeable or uneasy temper" (*Ibid.*, 31). Believing that man's primary goal in life was "the enjoyment of his God in a better world," (*Ibid.*, 4), England stressed that man could reach the goal only if he acknowledged his own dependency upon God, sought the will of God in the authoritative voice of the church, and lived a moral life. He emphasized, in particular, the bishops' authoritative tribunal; they were the only authentic interpreters of God's will (*Ibid.*, 37). The *Repertory* for 1814 and 1815 revealed that the times had changed, and England had changed with the times. The publication now stressed the active and social religious virtue of political resistance to the veto, rather than the passive and individualistic religious virtues of obedience and submission to one's state in life. England still advocated personal religious reformation through the periodical, but social and political reforms tended to dominate his thoughts. In fact, political reform, for him, was a manifestation of religious revival since it freed the church from governmental interference. Thus, during his clerical career in Ireland, England's mind on religious renewal was gradually, but definitely, transformed and broadened -- from one that was exclusively inward, individualistic and passive, to one that was outward, social and active.

EDUCATIONAL REFORMS

Religious reforms throughout Ireland were greatly supported by the simultaneous attempts to revitalize education. After the French Revolution, the movement for educational renewal was twofold: a program to establish seminaries for the education of a local clergy and an effort to construct facilities and programs for the education of the poor Irish Catholics. The establishment of facilities for the education of the Irish clergy at St. Patrick's College in Carlow in 1793 and at St.

Patrick's College in Maynooth in 1795 were events of major importance for the future of the Irish church.[50] Previous to this time the clergy were educated in Europe, primarily in France; therefore, they received their theology in cultures and in political milieu foreign to their own Irish environment. From 1793 on, the Irish clergy read their scriptures and their theology in light of their Irish circumstances. The "exclusively Irish experience" which the clergy received after 1793 has been called the "key factor in any understanding of the role of the priest in politics in nineteenth century Ireland" (O'Tuathaigh 1972: 47, 56). Bishop Doyle, who taught at Carlow from 1813 to 1819, often pointed out that the clerical training in Irish seminaries differed greatly from that on the continent, particularly in the area of political theory:

> This clergy, with few exceptions, are from the ranks
> of the people; they inherit their feelings; they are
> not, as formerly, brought up under despotic governments;
> they have imbibed the doctrines of Locke and Paley more
> deeply than those of Bellarmine or even of Bossuet on
> the divine right of kings; and they know much more of
> the principles of the constitution than they do of
> passive obedience.[51]

Political theory at Maynooth was likewise based upon Locke. The theory of the divine right of kings, according to one student in Maynooth, was held only by "an old superannuated Frenchman," and his opinion would have been received with "universal contempt" were he to have attempted to teach it at Maynooth.

> The prevailing opinion among Maynooth students on
> the subject of Government is that no particular
> form of Government is of Divine right; that the form
> of Government depends on the will and choice of the
> people, but that each is then strictly bound to support
> that form of Government as long as upheld by the
> people, and as long as he continues to live and seek
> for protection from that Government.[52]

Most of the text books used in the Irish seminaries were from the pen of "continental divines"; in theology, therefore, Doyle and a number of the Irish priests teaching in these seminaries found it necessary to adapt the continental ideas to the Irish experience (Fitzpatrick 1862: II, 76).

At times the Irish theologians differed greatly with the French theologians on points of doctrine and discipline (*Ibid.*, 89).

Some of the first teachers in the Irish seminaries were French emigré theologians who were said to be influenced by Gallicanism (Guilday 1927: I, 68). The teachers may have been Gallican, but there is little evidence to suggest, as some would have it,[53] that they influenced their Irish students in the Gallican traditions. In fact, the evidence is to the contrary. In politics, as well as in theology, the Irish began to develop their own positions in light of their own political-religious experiences. The Irish seminaries produced a new breed of priests with new political and theological views of church and state, freedom, and their own role in society (Gwynn 1929: 213, 216; *Works*, I, 206).

Although the education of the Irish clergy was successful upon the establishment of Irish seminaries, the instruction of the poor Irish-Catholic masses was neither as successful nor as easy to accomplish. Catholic participation in the teaching of the young had been legally prohibited by the penal system; even the 1782 relief act prohibited private individuals from giving funds for Catholic education. This act "had disastrous permanent effects in discouraging endowment of Catholic schools" (Corcoran 1928: xx). By 1824, according to a British Parliamentary report, there were 11,823 schools in Ireland, 46 of these were administered by sisters of various religious orders, 24 by the Christian Brothers, 352 by the Catholic clergy, and the remainder by numerous Protestant missionary and reform societies (MacCaffrey 1909: II, 221-22). Parliament-financed schools were almost exclusively the domain of the Protestant proselytizing societies during the eighteenth and early nineteenth centuries. When Count Montalembert visited Ireland in 1830 he drew a striking comparison between Protestant and Catholic educational conditions.

> Their [Protestant] school masters are well paid; a
> large and fine school is generally built at the side
> of the church, but the poor Catholics never send
> their children there. . . . And whilst their teacher
> dispatches the few children whom he has been enabled
> to collect, innumerable crowds press around the
> catholic priests, or the master to whom he pays a
> trifling salary, at the catholic chapel, or, perhaps,
> in the wretched barn, and frequently in a ditch
> scarcely sheltered by a thorn. There they are
> instructed in human science and the knowledge of
> God (Quoted in *USCM*, Feb. 15, 1834: 262).

Some of the most significant attempts to establish an educational system for the poor were centered in Cork. During the early nineteenth century, educational reform became a concern of the entire community of Cork -- Protestant as well as Catholic, laity as well as clergy. John England and many of the gentry and middle class believed that lack of education was a source of the social evils which afflicted the city; they held, for example, that it was a cause of some of the extreme poverty and rebellious tendencies of the poor (*CMC*, Feb. 12, 1812). England believed that good education was responsible for healing social wounds. He wrote in the *Chronicle*, July 19, 1815:

> Ever since a committee of Roman Catholics have been
> permitted to collect and to expend money in the
> instruction of the children of their communion, crime
> has diminished, morality has improved, social order has
> been ameliorated, and our city has exhibited an
> instance of peace, regularity, and good conduct, perhaps
> unrivalled not only in the United Kingdom but in Europe.

Educational reform was, therefore, for the benefit of society as well as for the welfare of the poorer classes. Catholics, who made up the vast majority of the poor, would not send their children to schools administered by Protestants and the Catholic clergy had neither sufficient funds nor personnel to administer enough schools for the poor Catholics. Education, therefore, had to be, in some way, separated from the exclusive control of Protestants. In view of this need, many Catholic and Protestant liberal-minded citizens invited the Englishman John Lancaster to Cork. Lancaster had been in the forefront of educational reform in England and was recognized by many in Cork, especially by John England, as the leading authority on the education of the poor. In the month of January, 1812, Lancaster came to Cork to deliver a number of lectures on his educational programs. According to an editorial in the *Chronicle*, Lancaster built his school system upon the concept of religious liberty which meant that education should be open to all "without religious distinction, and therefore was, as charity ever is, universal in its benevolent operation" (*CMC*, Jan. 31, 1812). Religious instruction, according to Lancaster, should not be used in the secular subjects (*CMC*, Feb. 14, 1812). This Lancaster principle of educational reform was hailed by many Protestants and Catholics in Cork.

After the lectures, a number of men of the city collected funds for building the first Lancaster school in Cork. The liberal contributions of prominent Protestants, especially William Beamish, helped to establish and support the school for the education of the poor of all religious denominations. Beamish was motivated, he said, by the desire to destroy bigotry and to engender in the young, kind feelings toward one another, regardless of their religious persuasion. These goals could be accomplished, he felt, if the children of all religious convictions were educated "under the one roof" (*CMC*, May 6, 1812). On May 4, 1812, foundations were laid for the school and it proved to be a successful first attempt at interdenominational education in Cork.

England became involved in these Cork educational reforms in three ways: by helping to establish a philosophy of education for the poor, by participating in the construction of poor schools, and by creating text books and simple readers for these schools. In 1812, he was appointed president of St. Mary's Theological Seminary in Cork and "superintendent" of education for the diocese of Cork. These new roles gave him a prominent position from which to organize education programs within the Catholic Church in Cork.

Sometime in 1814 or 1815, England helped to found a Catholic school for the poor. The school, called the Mardyke School, was established with the help of a committee of lay Catholics who were interested in the education of the poor Irish Catholics.[54] England administered the Mardyke School and utilized in part the Lancaster principles of education. He differed from Lancaster only in his belief that educational programs should include religious instruction. He believed in conducting religious education through the school system, but not through secular disciplines. In his school, therefore, all religious instruction was separated from the secular disciplines so that the school was opened to all of the poor of any religious persuasion. Parents were to choose whether or not they wanted their children to have religious instructions. If they did, they were to send them to school one hour before the secular lessons began.[55] According to England, "the will of the parent is perfect excuse" for the child's absence from religious education classes.[56] No one, England believed, should be in any way forced to receive religious instructions.[57]

England was involved in the publication of school texts as well as in constructing principles and programs for educational reform. He probably realized during his efforts to produce a religious literature that only a few of the "lower orders of society" could read the materials he produced. He, therefore, began to publish a number of elementary reading texts. One of his first publications, *Rudiments of Spelling and Reading*, was designed to help students learn the basic skills of reading. A second book, called the *Reading Book*, was a more advanced sequel to the first text.[58]

The *Reading Book* consisted primarily of simple stories on nature and the history of the lives of prominent Old and New Testament figures. The religious content of the book was amazingly non-denominational; it lacked all references to Catholicism or to any denominational strife in Ireland; it simply referred to God's Providence in nature and history. The variety of subject matter and the absence of denominational references made the book valuable for education at the time.[59]

By the time England left Ireland for the United States in 1820, ecclesiastical, moral and educational renewal was in the insecure and pilgrim state of an incipient movement. The three different but interrelated church reforms, much like those in the political realm, achieved only limited success during the period 1800 to 1820. They were more valuable in identifying the church with the forces for change, laying a foundation for later ecclesiastical regeneration, and establishing a reform mentality among many of the bishops, priests and laity than they were in actually transforming the church. John England's participation in the political and ecclesiastical movements gave him not only a reform mentality, but also an experience in organizing democratic political pressure groups. He learned, moreover, the value of cooperative efforts between the laity and the clergy in effecting political, social and religious changes as well as the necessity of a nationally and locally organized church to manifest unity and achieve reform. Furthermore, he gained an understanding of world politics, and imbibed a positive attitude to the changing events of the contemporary world.

The most effective and lasting reform of the period was the evolution of a strong national and local episcopal structure. Second in importance to the formation of the episcopacy was the establishment of the native seminaries. Both of these developments strengthened the Irish church and helped to build a sense of a national Irish Catholic Church. These two major achievements of the age were more the result of external, political forces than they were of internal ecclesiastical design; however, they were also the consequence of perceptive ecclesiastical responses to those changing political conditions.

The ecclesiastical as well as the political reforms were intended to change the religious and political life of the Irish Catholic people. They were, moreover, motivated by political and religious ideals and ideologies which were articulately developed and expressed in the public press, in personal letters, and in a few studies on specific contemporary political and ecclesiastical problems. Those ideals and ideologies are outlined in the next chapter.

SECTION II

---

an irish catholic intellectual tradition

When many historians study the development of Catholic thought in the late eighteenth and early nineteenth centuries, they rarely analyze Irish Catholic thought; rather, they look to France or Germany for critical developments or for the dominant pattern of theological intransigence. Thus, they conclude that throughout the nineteenth century the Roman Catholic Church was almost unalterably opposed "to liberalizing trends, intellectual or political" (Reardon 1966: 30). When they do study Irish Catholicism during this period they judge that the Irish contributed greatly to the physical and numerical growth of Catholicism in the diaspora churches outside of Ireland, but that they developed "nothing . . . in terms of thought and devotional life" (Latourette 1958: I, 451).

A closer examination of the veto controversy and other developments in the Irish church balances the almost universal view of the Catholic Church's resistance to liberalizing trends at this period. The veto contentions, as the French Revolution and other European upheavals, raised a number of significant questions about the role of authority in political and ecclesiastical life: What was the foundation of authentic civil and religious liberty? What was the precise relationship of the church to the state? Was voluntaryism necessary, or would state support be better for the church's survival? What was the church's role in the changing political climate of the period? At the beginning of the nineteenth century, as one observer has noted, the Catholic Church in Europe (and in Ireland, we might add) hardly knew where she stood in regard to these questions (Hales 1960: 12).

While responding to these problems, the anti-vetoist leaders of the Irish controversy developed and formulated "liberal" views on religious liberty, the separation of church and state, voluntaryism in religion, and the mission of the church in a new age. Irish Catholic liberalism, however, was never identified with the liberalism of the French Revolution (Coldrick 1974: 209; *USCM*, Dec. 5, 1829: 180). In fact, the Irish liberals frequently noted that liberalism in Ireland was nonviolent; it was a mass democratic movement in favor of the civil and religious rights of all peoples; it was based on universal charity. They claimed that the Irish Catholic Church was on the side of the people and on the side of liberty -- unlike Catholicism in France and Protestantism in Ireland, both of which were enemies of the people and freedom (Coldrick 1974: 200). Thus, the liberals certainly did not see any incompatibility between their advocacy of freedom and their faith in Catholicism. In fact, they saw liberalism as part of their Catholic heritage.

The early nineteenth-century liberals expressed publicly ideas which seem to have been silently developing for a century within the individual and collective Irish consciousness. Their views had roots in the common Irish Catholic historical experiences and in the theological traditions of the late eighteenth-century polemics. The liberals can be adequately understood only within this context. Section II, therefore, delineates briefly the views of Arthur O'Leary, Daniel O'Connell, Bishop James Doyle, and others in the Irish tradition; second, it focuses upon the ideas of John England. The developing Irish Catholic tradition provides the proper context for perceiving England's liberalism.

Arthur O'Leary, the Cork cleric, Daniel O'Connell, the national Liberator, and James Warren Doyle, the famous JKL (James, Bishop of Kildare and Leighlin), have been chosen as representatives of the liberal views because their ideas seem to have been characteristic of the mentality of a large segment of Irish Catholic society and because they were the most articulate national leaders of this tradition. John England's perceptions are important not only because he was a leader on the local level in Ireland, but also because he illustrated and represented the ease with which the Irish immigrant adjusted to American political and religious experiences and adapted liberal Irish views to American conditions.

CHAPTER I

---

religious liberty

The issue of religious liberty, which had dominated the Irish Catholic emancipation movement in the late eighteenth century, was the first question raised during the veto controversy. Did the state have a right to impose civil disabilities or even favors upon a person or religious community because of their religious beliefs. The response to the question, as we have already seen, evolved out of the historical experience of Irish Catholicism. The Irish advocacy of religious freedom was based not only upon justified self-interest, but also upon religious and political principles.

Although the liberals' profession of religious liberty appealed to Irish Catholic self-interest, nevertheless it applied to all who suffered discrimination on the grounds of religious beliefs or worship. From the time of Arthur O'Leary's first public appearances in the 1780's, many of the Irish had discussed the Christian principles which supported the movement for civil and religious liberty. In 1781, while preparing an edition of a series of essays on religious toleration, O'Leary wrote:

> In the course of this work, I intend to make Toleration
> a citizen of the world, instead of confining it to one
> kingdom or province. I am not an able, neither am I a

partial advocate. I plead for the Protestant in France,
and for the Jew in Lisbon, as well as for the Catholic
in Ireland (O'Leary 1781: xv).

In 1822, Thomas England, O'Leary's biographer and John England's
brother, commented on O'Leary's "Essay on Toleration":

Never were the grounds on which rests the inalienable
right possessed by every man to worship God, uncontrolled
by human legislation so far as regards speculative opinions,
more clearly stated or more ably enforced, than in this
essay (T. England 1822: 97).

According to Thomas England, O'Leary's essay had a circulation
"almost unequalled" during the early nineteenth century in Ireland
(*Ibid.*, 99).

Like O'Leary, Daniel O'Connell supported the principle of religious
liberty and universal toleration. O'Connell first spoke on religious
liberty in 1807 when he told a meeting of Catholics in Dublin that he
placed the Catholic claims for emancipation "on the new score of
justice -- of that justice which would emancipate the Protestant in
Spain and Portugal, the Christian in Constantinople" as well as the
Catholic in Ireland (*The Correspondent*, a Dublin newspaper, March
5, 1807, quoted in M. O'Connell 1975: 180). On February 23, 1814,
O'Connell repeated the principle -- as he would do many times in his·
career. He advocated

the eternal right to freedom of conscience -- a right
which, I repeat it with pride and pleasure, would
exterminate the Inquisition in Spain and bury in oblivion
the bloody orange flag of dissension in Ireland (J. O'Connell
1867: II, 16; See also *CMC*, Sept. 5, 1813).

For John England, as for O'Leary and O'Connell, religious liberty
was universal. It applied not only to Irish Catholics, but also to
Protestants, Jews, Moslems and every other religious denomination. In
Cork, England supported a number of petitions that were directed
toward the religious liberty of various denominations throughout the
world. On April 19, 1816, for example, he signed resolutions of the
Cork Catholic Aggregate meeting which protested the "cruel persecution of the Protestants in France." The resolution read:

> That unalterably attached to the principles of Religious
> Liberty, and sympathising with those who suffer on the
> score of conscience, we would deem ourselves unworthy
> of that Freedom, which as Irishmen and Catholics, we
> demand, did we not thus publicly express our unqualified
> abhorence, and detestation of the late cruel persecution
> of the Protestants in France, a persecution as inconsistent
> with every principle of justice, and liberal policy, as contrary
> to the sacred and inalienable rights of humanity.[1]

The civil liberties they wanted for themselves, the Irish also desired for
all humanity. They advocated liberties for the negro slave; but they
protested that those who fought so hard in England for the full civil
freedom of the negro slave were inconsistent because these same persons sought to continue the oppression of the "White Slave of our country" (CMC, June 24, 1814; see also July 1 and 4, 1814).

England repeatedly used the practice of religious liberty in the
United States as an ideal example for the world to follow. America was
the place where Christianity "is spreading together with freedom and
civilization" (CMC, March 11, 1816). Because of this, "even" the
American lawyer could "boast of the superiority of his code when compared to ours, upon Religious subjects" (CMC, June 7, 1815). The
decisions of the American courts on religious subjects likewise
manifested the superior wisdom of American jurisprudence" (Repertory, III, 28).

In the course of his ministry in Ireland, England participated in a
number of reform programs to advance religious liberty. We have
already seen his involvement in the veto question and his participation
in educational reform as manifestations of that concern. In addition,
from 1810 to 1817, as chaplain to the Catholic prisoners in Cork,
England struggled to promote religious liberty in the prison system of
that county. A number of rules had greatly limited the prisoners' access
to their clergymen. On May 27, 1816, after years of attempting to
bring about some change in these local regulations, England petitioned
the Lord Lieutenant of Ireland, Earl Whitworth, to "enable Roman
Catholic prisoners to enjoy that liberty of conscience which alone can
make the practices of Religion meritorious, and that intercourse with
their clergyman which will reduce the principle to practice" (CMC,
May 31, 1816). The appeal was successful and all the obstacles were
removed on May 29, 1816.

England based his support for religious liberty on his understanding
of the natural rights of man and the nature of Christian faith and

charity. For him, religious freedom was simply a God-given gift every man should enjoy by virtue of his human nature. Religious liberty was the right every person possessed to entertain his own religious convictions, to express and propagate them publicly, to belong to the religious denomination of his choice, and not to suffer any civil, temporal or corporeal disabilities either as an individual or as a member of a religious society because of such personal or corporate behavior (*CMC*, April 29, 1816). Religious beliefs and their expressions could be justly oppressed by the civil arm only when they destroyed social order.

England also based religious freedom upon the fact that faith was free and the church was a voluntary institution; no temporal force, therefore, should be used to change, promote or sustain religious opinions. England believed that the British Government's offer to pay the clergy's salaries in exchange for the veto was one form of temporal influence upon religion. No religious person, he stated, should be subjected to such temporal *quid pro quo* arrangements. He suspected that ultimately such privileges would be used to alter a person's religion (*CMC*, Dec. 8, 1815). No matter what the ultimate purpose may have been, however, the church should never be tempted by such offerings because its mission to the world stood on its own spiritual resources and not upon governmental aid. The church, founded by Jesus Christ, should follow his example in announcing truth to the world. Jesus was no bigot: "He taught truth, and gained converts by persuasion."[2] He used no temporal pains or penalties in order to persuade his followers of the truth of his message and the divine foundation of his mission. Like him, the church had the responsibility to use spiritual means to promote and sustain the faith. If a minister should find anyone in error, he should follow the divine Master's example and "endeavour to reclaim him by argument and by persuasion" (*CMC*, Sept. 5, 1814).

England found another basis for religious liberty in the gospel principle of universal charity. All men were to be respected and tolerated regardless of their religious opinions and beliefs. Toleration was one of the highest Christian virtues since it was based upon love of neighbor.[3] Charity meant that every Christian had the duty to respect each man's God-given right to believe and to express what he considered to be true; no Christian could justly impose any temporal or spiritual suffering on a man because of his convictions and religious expressions (*CMC*, April 26, 1816).

Religious liberty, however, was not religious indifference. Every person had the responsibility to search for the truth and to preserve it when he found it. He did not have a license to believe whatever suited his fancy or whatever was most useful. England argued against those who used the rubric of "liberty of conscience" as a pretext for their own personal whims.

> You might often find in one family as many religions as
> there were individuals who composed it. The pretext
> and apology for all this were liberty of conscience
> and the privilege of general toleration. In reality,
> nothing is more flattering to self-love and vanity, than
> to judge for one's self, to assume the Ephod, and to be
> the arbiter of our own belief (*Repertory*, III, 15).

Freedom of conscience, for England, had to be balanced with a love of authority and a dependence upon it. Only a bigot, he noted, was unreasonably wedded to an opinion for which he could neither show the authority of God nor the force of reason. A man's liberty was not absolute. A responsible freedom acknowledged the limitations of the human mind and adhered to the just decisions of constituted authority. For Catholics, therefore, a man's independence was limited by the boundaries of revelation as authentically interpreted by the general body of bishops (*Repertory*, II, 33). In all other matters not defined by this body of bishops, a Catholic was free to hold opinions which he found to be reasonable.

Religious liberty, for England, was inherent in human nature, the personal act of faith, the natural limitations of temporal government, the voluntary nature of the church, and the universal law of love of neighbor. It was a negative principle in that it forbade political interference in the rights of a religious conscience; but it was also a positive principle in that it acknowledged that religious communities as well as individuals had rights in society -- i.e., religion was not merely a private affair.

CHAPTER II

---

separation of church and state

The issue of religious liberty naturally led to its corollary, separation of church and state. The veto controversy raised the question of the proper relationship between the church and the state, between the spiritual and temporal powers in any society. As we have seen, the Irish Catholics' historical experience taught them to abhor the union of church and state and to value separation as an ideal; now the ideological development of the principle of separation must be examined.

Although the Irish-Catholic ideology on the separation of church and state arose most forcefully, most publicly and most effectively during the veto controversy (1808-1816), the roots of the Irish tradition lie in the late eighteenth century. The tradition developed when Irish Catholic apologists attempted to answer Protestant theological objections to Catholic emancipation. The British Government and many Irish and English Protestants rejected political and religious freedom for Catholics on the grounds that the Catholics could not be good citizens because of their religion. The Protestants believed that because the Catholic was united to the papacy, a foreign power which had the authority to depose kings, he could not be a good subject of the king (Beckett 1966: 296). Furthermore, Catholic theologians and councils in the past had approved the doctrine that a Catholic did not have to keep faith with heretics; therefore, Catholic oaths of loyalty to the government could not be considered valid because they could be revoked by the will of the pope or by a general church council.

In 1757, the Irish Catholic Association gave one of the first major public statements in response to these charges. Under the leadership of James O'Keefe, Catholic Bishop of Kildare and Leighlin, the Association issued a declaration on the relationship of the Catholic Church to the state. The members declared that no doctrine in the Catholic Church recognized any right or power of deposing sovereigns, absolving subjects from their oaths, making war upon heretics, or exercising any temporal power or jurisdiction in Ireland. They also denied that the infallibility of the pope was a Catholic doctrine, and swore that as Catholics they were loyal subjects to the king and would do nothing to disturb or weaken the government, property or the religion of the established church.[4] An oath of political allegiance containing similar sentiments was drawn up by the Catholic committee -- a body of lay gentry and merchants -- in 1772 and submitted to Rome; it later became the basis of the 1774 oath, which the Irish Parliament approved and which the lay Catholic landowners and some Irish bishops took to prove their loyalty to the British government (*Works*, II, 230). Similar declarations were drawn up in 1792; these formulations, in John England's words, were "consonant to what always was the Catholic doctrine" (*Works*, II, 418). In order to prove their allegiance to the British Crown, Catholics abjured the charges against them and in the process showed that they believed in a separation of the spiritual and temporal powers in every society. This was not, however, a declaration of the doctrine of the separation of church and state.

The theological difficulties Irish and English Catholics faced stemmed in part from Bellarmine's theology of the pope's indirect deposing power and the Protestant understanding of the Fourth Lateran Council's (1215) third decree.[5] During the eighteenth century, Father Arthur O'Leary, the champion of Irish Catholic loyalty to the British Government, was the strongest opponent of Bellarmine's theology of the pope's deposing power. He felt that Bellarmine and like-minded persons were activated by "an excessive veneration for the first pastor of the church" (O'Leary 1871: 117). Bellarmine, O'Leary argued, was only an individual, and therefore he could not speak for the entire church; he could in no way declare personal opinion to be church doctrine. O'Leary's famous phrase against Bellarmine: "Must an Irish Catholic starve, because an Italian wrote nonsense in bad Italian (*sic*) two hundred years ago?" was frequently repeated in the Irish emancipation movement (*Ibid.*, 134). O'Leary held that the pope had no direct or indirect authority in temporal affairs. Other Irish Catholics who sought political and religious liberation continually denied Bellarmine's "excessive" admiration for papal prerogatives. Bishop

James Doyle and a host of other Irish liberators agreed with Daniel O'Connell's sentiments: "I am sincerely a Catholic, but I am not a Papist. I deny the doctrine that the Pope has any temporal authority, directly or indirectly, in Ireland."[6]

Perhaps the strongest argument against Catholic loyalty to a Protestant government came from the third decree of the Fourth Lateran Council. The decree gave the church the power to exterminate heretics and absolve subjects from their oaths of allegiance to heretical governments. Most Irish Catholic apologists claimed that the decree had to be read within its historical context. During the medieval period, they argued, church and state were united -- so much so that kings and governments had consented to give the pope and the church, authority which the church did not possess under its spiritual constitution. The pope, therefore, was considered a temporal as well as a spiritual lord. As such, he could interfere in secular as well as ecclesiastical affairs. Many of the decrees of the medieval councils, therefore, had to be seen as purely temporal measures of discipline and not doctrines of the church. Such was the Lateran decree; it was a reflection of the religio-politico circumstances of medieval Christendom. According to Doyle, it had no permanent effect -- particularly during the early nineteenth century, because the political climate had completely changed and because the law had been abrogated simply by disuse. According to Bishop Doyle, expressing the position held by Catholic apologists,

> Such a law in the present age...would be immoral,
> unjust, impossible; it would be opposed to the natural
> dispositions of the people of this empire; it would be
> contrary to all the laws, usages and customs, of our
> country; it would not be suited to the times and
> circumstances in which we live; in place of being
> necessary and useful, it would upturn the very
> foundations of society; and instead of benefiting
> the entire community, it would drench our streets
> and our fields in blood (Doyle 1826: 110-11).

In a word, Doyle noted, such legislation violated Gratian's principles of law.

The Irish leaders' denial of "excessive" papal prerogatives and their interpretation of Lateran IV's third decree manifested their belief in the separation of spiritual and temporal powers. Gradually, this tenet became a cornerstone for the doctrine of the separation of church and state. As shall be demonstrated, their conviction was not based simply upon historical expediency; it was grounded in Christian principles. For Arthur O'Leary, as for many of the Irish-Catholic leaders, the separation of church and state was part of Christ's original plan. "The Spirit of Christ abhors the intrusion of temporal powers into the sanctuary of religion" (T. England 1822: 96). Likewise, the interference of the spiritual authority of the church, directly or indirectly, in the affairs of the state was contrary to the design of Christ. The spiritual and the temporal powers were given two distinct arenas of life to govern. They were not to be mixed, nor were they to be confused. Temporal governments were organized to protect the human and civil rights of men (i.e., those of life, liberty, and the power to accumulate a fortune by honest means), prerogatives derived from human nature. Civil rulers had no inherent power to deny or reverse these natural privileges; in fact, by the "social compact" civil rulers were bound to protect them; if they violated these claims they did so "by a stretch of power, not by the rule of right."[7] As the secular government had responsibility for the temporal concerns of mankind, so the church was accountable for spiritual welfare and could use only moral means of persuasion to accomplish its ends. According to O'Leary, therefore, the two governments could flourish only when they were free from each other's interference; they survived best in separation.

Thomas Hussey (1741-1803), Bishop of Waterford, followed in O'Leary's footsteps in maintaining the necessity of an absolute separation of the powers of the church and the state. In his pastoral letter of 1796, he wrote:

> In all temporal matters they [Catholics] are subject to
> their temporal rulers -- in all spiritual matters, they
> are subject to their spiritual rulers. These two
> authorities, like parallel lines in mathematics, can never
> touch each other. By the smallest declination, they
> lose even their names (Pastoral in *Repertory*, II, 489).

Daniel O'Connell was in the same Irish tradition. In 1815 he laid down the principle of the separation of church and state as the foundation for the opposition to the veto:

> Let us also advocate our cause on the two great
> principles -- first, that of an eternal separation
> in spirituals between our church and the state;
> secondly, that of the eternal right to freedom of
> conscience.[8]

In 1830, in the context of the French Revolution of that year, O'Connell made his position on the principle of separation even more forceful. "There is one feature in this great and satisfactory change which I hail with the most profound conviction of utility -- the complete severance of the church from the state" (M. O'Connell 1972-   : IV, Letter 1709, quoted in M. O'Connell 1975: 182). Upon this principle, O'Connell led the opposition to British and Roman intervention in Irish affairs. On the one hand, he opposed Roman involvement in the veto because he felt it was an interference in the struggle of Irish Catholics to secure their political prerogatives. Rome had no right to intercede for Catholics in their campaign for political emancipation. On the other hand, he objected to the British Government's attempt to obtain the veto because it had no business meddling in the spiritual concerns of Roman Catholics. The nomination of bishops was, for him, a matter of internal local church discipline.[9]

Bishop Doyle also advocated a separation of church and state; he based his call upon the demands of the times and the "nature of government" (Doyle 1823: 37). The entire world had changed, according to Doyle. New political ideas, new constitutions, new relationships between the governor and the governed had developed. These changes alone would demand a separation. People no longer lived in the world of medieval Christendom, and to preserve the medieval state of laws and constitutions was contrary to the times.

> The whole civil constitution of Europe is new-modelled
> -- the ideas of men have undergone an entire revolution --
> the relative situation of princes and popes is changed
> altogether -- the influence of the papal authority in
> things temporal, is neither feared nor felt anywhere,
> because it does not exist (*Ibid.*, 28).

If an analysis of the contemporary political situation were not enough to reveal the necessity of separation, the nature of government itself would be sufficient. Quoting Montesquieu, Doyle maintained that good government adjusted its laws to fit the temper, habits, traditions, resources, modes of industry and religion of its inhabitants (Doyle 1825: 88). The present state of government in Ireland, the union of the Anglican Church with the state, in no way reflected this description of good government.

Doyle argued, furthermore, that "all religions are indifferent to the constitution."[10] The civil constitution of any government was not a religious but a social compact. "There are two contracting parties, the individual and the society, [sic,] both are independent, free, and possessed of something valuable, for which, on contracting, each requires a consideration." By its very nature it was wrong for a government to demand religious oaths and allegiances. Such requirements could only have arisen "from certain accidental or temporary occurrences" (Doyle 1825: 237); they were not part of the social compact.

According to Doyle, the separation of church and state was also based upon the source of the state's authority. The state, whatever form it assumed, received its power from the people and ultimately from God; as a result it was completely independent from the pope, from any church, or from any other authority, except that which "the constitution itself..., may recognize as an immediate basis or source of its own power."[11] The state, in fact, "does not need the aid of the church, unless to teach morality to the people" (Doyle 1823: 38).

The Cork anti-vetoists, and John England in particular, followed in the footsteps of their national spokesmen on the question of the relationship between church and state. They were not completely dependent upon them, however, for their views. In fact, John England warned the Corkmen that even O'Connell, the principal national spokesman, was too "unsuspecting" of the Catholic vetoists.[12] England believed that O'Connell and other national leaders were at times willing to make concessions to the Catholic vetoists in order to create harmony in the Catholic community, thereby forging a stronger Catholic unity in the struggle for emancipation. England, however, demanded unqualified emancipation; one could not relax the principle of separation of church and state for the sake of momentary peace within the community. He did not swerve from this principle throughout his life.[13]

In the process of opposing the veto, England revealed his arguments for preserving a separation of the Irish Church from the British Government. He based his case upon his understanding of the nature of state government, the mission of the church, scriptural precept, preservation of the Irish tradition, historical experience and the propensities of a weak human nature.

England's perception of the role of government demanded a separation of religious and civil jurisdiction. The state had its origin and foundation in the sovereignty of the people. They were the source of all government and of every constitution, even though God as creator was the ultimate cause. The responsibility of civil authority, therefore, was to provide for the temporal welfare of all its citizens, without regard for religious distinctions, because as citizens, all were equal. "We may in the intercourse of civil life, forget the distinctions of

Religion, and look upon every child of Adam as a brother" (*CMC*, April 26, 1816). Since God had given men the rights of civil and religious freedom, "no man has therefore, a right to give me the alternative of civil liberty or religious opinion" (*CMC*, April 23, 1817). A government of men, no matter how constituted, did not have the license to take from men what God had bestowed upon them. It had no right to restrict civil liberties because of one's religious convictions or practices; it had no jurisdiction except over the temporal affairs of men. Because of its very nature, every government had strict limits to its powers. In this regard, England considered the American Constitution and jurisprudence to be superior to that of many of the constitutions and juridical decisions of Europe.[14] The American legal system had provided for the civil liberties of all without infringing upon religious opinions.

The separation of church and state, according to England, was also grounded in the nature of the church. "The Church is purely a spiritual society," England wrote in 1815, "whose laws by no means regard concerns purely temporal and civil" (*Repertory*, II, 152). The pope, in particular, had no right to infringe upon the civil liberties of any Irish citizens. One of the criticisms that could be made "upon the former inhabitants of Ireland, is, that they allowed Adrian to sell them to Henry" (*CMC*, Aug. 21, 1815). Cardinal Consalvi -- "the Papa Rosa," as England called him -- was criticized in this regard as "the worst Divine in the Sacred College" because he tried to increase the pope's temporal influence by obtaining the veto for the British Government (*CMC*, March 29, 1816). The church was supernatural and had spiritual functions; the state was secular and had temporal duties. The two should not interfere in each other's missions; to do so would be to violate their own natures.

England also used the command of Christ to support his opposition to the veto and his advocacy of separation. In an 1814 conference of the clergy of the diocese of Cork, England prepared the following resolution which was signed by sixty Cork clergymen:

> Thus manifesting our adherence to the Divine Precept,
> of giving unto Caesar the things which are Caesar's,
> and of giving unto God the things which are God's..:
> we will, under all circumstances...uniformly, from
> principle [oppose state interference in ecclesiastical
> matters] (*CMC*, May 20, 1814).

If the papacy or the government were to impose the veto on Irish-Catholics, England believed that the Irish should resist on the grounds that "God is to be obeyed, rather than man" (*CMC*, Sept. 29, 1813). England and the Irish Catholics used the gospel command to confirm and preserve their historical experience of separation.

The Irish Catholic forefathers, England further maintained, had taught the Catholics of Ireland to keep the church and state separate. The Irish Catholic Church was free and independent, when it remained unattached to the state, even though it suffered from poverty. To give up that independence by submission to the veto would be to violate those long dead who had preserved Catholic freedom in the past at the cost of their property, their wealth, their honor, at times even their families and their very lives (*CMC*, June 16, 1813). The Irish Catholic had a proud tradition of separation to maintain. Thus, anti-vetoism in England's opinion was a conservative movement -- a campaign to preserve Irish tradition.

Historical experience and human weakness had also taught England that the state did not grant favors without expecting reciprocation. The Irish clergy, in England's words, "saw the connection which the state would claim with their church and they thought it dangerous and alarming; they wished to keep them separate" (*CMC*, June 6, 1814). Even though the vetoist protested that the state desired no influence over the church, that it wanted only to secure social and civil tranquility by the veto, still England opposed the measure because historically the promises of civil leaders had often been contradicted by actions. "We should take lessons of caution," he wrote, "from the records of history, and learn the dispositions of men rather from their acts than from their profession" (*CMC*, Aug. 18, 1815). Once before, in 1799, the bishops had been promised emancipation for their agreement to the Union; the Union, however, was accomplished without it. One could not now believe that the church would remain free from lay or government interference if the veto were granted.[15]

Uniting the church and the state in Ireland by granting the state the power of the veto over the nomination of Irish bishops was considered the first step in destroying Catholicism in Ireland. Vetoists, like Cardinal Consalvi, claimed that this would not happen. According to England, Consalvi told Richard Hayes that if the pope granted the veto "God would take care of the consequence." When vetoists argued that God's providence would care for the church until the end of time, England countered that God's promise did not guarantee "to any particular nation the possession of the true faith uninterruptedly." The life span of the church in North Africa, England maintained, should illustrate that God's universal providence did not always protect the particular church from extinction. Man could not presumptuously forfeit his responsibility for the preservation of the local church on the grounds that God would sustain it. In the case of the veto, one could not gamble that the church would not be annihilated in Ireland; therefore, all persons had the responsibility to oppose the veto because it would probably destroy Catholic religion in Ireland. The safest and surest course for any Irish Catholic, therefore, was to reject the union of church and state because of its possible future consequences (*CMC*, March 11, 1816).

Some vetoists, including Pope Pius VII, had argued that granting the veto in Ireland was not an essential change in the faith, government or general discipline of the church; it was only a matter of modifying specific local church discipline. The anti-vetoists, like England, responded that religion itself was the citadel and its discipline was its outposts. In order to protect the citadel, one also had to defend the outposts. Discipline in the local church was of extreme importance because it "reduces the doctrine of Religion to practice." It was the necessary link between the Catholic and his religion, whereby he came into contact with the incomprehensible mysteries of his faith; it was the "essential medium of communion betwixt God and man"; to destroy it or change it would endanger the connection. Any concession in this matter would fundamentally compromise religion (*CMC*, Sept. 29, 1813).

Although England and the Cork anti-vetoists argued against state involvement in religious affairs and for a continued separation of church and state, they acknowledged that the union of church and state did exist and could continue in other countries without the destruction of the faith. But even where this alliance had taken place, the constitution and essence of the church had not been changed. The church was still a spiritual reality and no union could destroy that nature. Even though the church aligned with the state, "it is plain that the civil power and the ecclesiastical power are quite distinct but not opposed" (*Repertory*, II, 152). Even in an historical union of church and state, a theoretical distinction between the two remained. Although separation was not considered an absolute, for England and the Cork Catholics, it was the historical ideal. The Irish liberals interpreted the traditional distinction between the spiritual and the temporal in light of their experience, and applied that distinction to the existing separation of the Irish Catholic Church from the British government; in view of their historical environment, therefore, they gave new meaning to the traditional concept.

CHAPTER III

---

voluntaryism

The third major question during the veto controversy concerned the provision in Grattan's bill on the state payment of the clergy. The anti-vetoists objected to this proposal on the grounds that the church could remain free when it relied only on the free will offerings of the laity rather than on the financial support of the state.[16]

The anti-vetoists used their own Irish experience of voluntaryism to oppose state payment of the clergy.[17] The Irish Catholic Church's separation from the British government forced the Catholic Church to rely almost exclusively upon the free-will offerings of the laity to maintain and support the clerical ministry and the few religious institutions it possessed. This experience gave John England and some of the anti-vetoists sufficient reason to justify the idea and practice of voluntaryism as a religious ideal.

According to England, the Irish Catholic clergy were sustained in the past by the liberality of their people and they did not want nor would they consent to any change in a practice that had created bonds of intimate friendship and "fellow-feeling" between the priests and the people (*CMC*, May 10, 1813). They desired no state payment of the clergy because they wanted no conflicts between their duties to religion and their obligations to the state. If the clergy acquiesced to state aid, they would thereby create for themselves vested interests in the state and could not be solely concerned about the people's welfare. According to England, the clergy felt the need to maintain a critical distance from the state even in the area of their financial support. When the vetoists objected to anti-vetoists' arguments by saying "rely on your own integrity," England responded: "we will not put ourselves in the way of temptation" (*CMC*, June 6, 1814). For England, the vetoists had underestimated the weakness of human nature and had not perceived the historical evils that resulted from the state payment of the clergy. The clergy of the Established Church and even the Presbyterian ministers under state payment had bartered and forfeited the rights of the Irish people in exchange for a life of comfort and ease. The Irish Catholic clergy, according to England, preferred the poverty and oppression of the religion of Jesus to the luxury of a state-supported religion.

> The clergy ask for no riches, no power, no advantages,
> -- all they want is, that the faith preserved by their
> predecessors amidst every oppression and penalty, shall
> be protected from ministerial or political influence at
> present.[18]

The long history of British oppression made some of the clergy and laity suspicious of all state offers to support the Catholic religion; they saw governmental plans, in all their subtle forms, as an attempt to destroy their religion. England and many of the anti-vetoists, therefore, rejected state support; voluntaryism, they thought, was more in accord with the religion of Jesus than was governmental care of the church.

Because of their own historical circumstances and experiences, O'Leary, O'Connell, Doyle, England and many of the Irish emphasized the subjective nature of religion in their call for civil and religious liberty. Governmental persecution of Catholicism had taught them to value the inner truth of every man's voluntary convictions. They could see themselves as convinced Catholics, and yet could tolerate the different beliefs of others. England's personal experience, in particular, drove him to search the records of Christian revelation and tradition in order to formulate a Catholic position on religious liberty, separation of church and state, and voluntaryism. Experience and the Christian heritage, therefore, worked together in building an Irish Catholic enthusiasm for these principles.

CHAPTER IV

---

church

The fourth principal issue raised during the veto controversy involved the nature of the church. Two separate questions were raised: The first concerned the rights and duties of the national Irish episcopacy in reference to the Roman papacy. In essence, the problem centered on the relationship between the national and universal church. It arose because of the growing sense of Irish Nationalism, but it was brought into focus primarily because of papal interference in the veto controversy. When personnel in the papal courts, and later the pope himself, tried to encourage the Irish and English Catholics to accept the veto, the anti-vetoist liberals responded by trying to clarify the nature of the national church and the rights of the local episcopacy in relationship to the papacy. The second question pertained to the nature of the roles of bishop, priest and layman within the national church. It arose primarily because some of the vetoists objected to the involvement of priests and laity in issues which they felt belonged exclusively to the domain of the bishops. While responding to this objection, the anti-vetoists presented their views on the nature of the different roles within the church.

THE NATIONAL CHURCH AND THE PAPACY

The Irish anti-vetoists objected to Roman intervention in Irish ecclesiastical affairs on the grounds that it violated the "rights of our
National Church."[19] John England defended these prerogatives in four
ways: he showed the constitutional relationship between the
episcopacy and the papacy; presented the legal limits of papal power;
outlined the practical limitations of papal competence; and affirmed
the constitutional responsibility of the local episcopacy.

Before one can understand John England's approach to the relationship between the episcopacy and the papacy, one must understand his
overall constitutional view of the ecclesiastical community. For him,
the church's constitution was a "purely spiritual reality" and,
therefore, could not be equated with political constitutions. Unlike
secular governments, the church was an historical community of persons with divinely defined and limited constitutional roles, duties,
powers, and rights. Although England delineated the essential differences between ecclesiastical and political constitutions, he nevertheless continually compared the similarities between the Catholic
Church's constitution and that of the British Government. For him, the
church was also a human community -- analogous to the political.

The church was a mixed government like that of Great Britain. The
similarity of the two forms of government was not simply the result of
coincidence; according to England, many believed that the "legislative
perfection" of the Catholic Church was the prototype of the British
constitution. Although he acknowledged the differences between the
king and the pope, England frequently compared their office and
duties. The king had his privy counsellors; the pope had his cardinals.
Governors who ruled under the king were likened to the bishops. As the
Empire was divided into kingdoms and provinces, so the church was
divided into provinces and dioceses. Mayors, sheriffs and constables
were compared to deans, archdeacons and parish priests. Parliament
was similar to the general councils in that the assent of these bodies
must be obtained to make general statutes or define articles of faith.
The peers and commons corresponded to the bishops and priests; peers,
like bishops, formed a judicial tribunal -- the one by hereditary
privilege the other by divine right; law, like scripture, needed to be interpreted. The voice of Parliament, like the voice of a general council,
had the definitive role of interpretation. No appeal was possible
beyond the decisions of either Parliament and king, or those of pope

and general council. Felony, like heresy, was a crime, and treason, like schism, was the full renunciation of constituted authority.[20] England believed that his comparison of the constitution of the Catholic Church to that of the British Government had all the weaknesses of an analogy. It broke down in two places in particular: first, the church was spiritual and the state temporal; secondly, the church was not democratic: "Be not astonished at the comparison for the boasted constitution of England, from which Catholics are excluded, is, with the exception of its democratic part, modelled upon our church government."[21] England's comparison of the church's constitution to that of the state put him in the habit of perceiving the church in light of political principles and practices.

England's view of the church helped him to see Rome's intervention in Irish church discipline as a constitutional consideration. The veto crisis, somewhat like the conciliarists' struggles of the fifteenth century, raised two major questions on the proper limitations of powers within the church: (1) Could the pope change the local discipline of the church of Ireland against the will of its bishops? (2) If the bishops refused to comply with the pope's attempt to modify that discipline were they schismatic? England maintained that he could find no theologians who had treated these specific subjects. The questions, he maintained, had to be answered on the basis of a proper understanding of the nature of church government.

According to England, both the papacy and the episcopacy were of "divine right." The source and foundation of these powers in the church were found in apostolic succession.

> The ordinary Apostolic power is lodged in the successors
> of the Apostles, upon whom our Lord bestowed it, and
> their successors are his Holiness, as successor to St.
> Peter, the Prince of the Apostles and Head of the
> Church, and the Bishops of the special place, as the
> successors to the particular Apostles of that place,
> and who therefrom have ordinary jurisdiction therein
> (*CMC*, May 18, 1814).

Those divinely-established papal and episcopal powers, however, had proper limitations which were very much like the constitutional restraints of power in the British form of government. Both the Catholic Church and the British government were limited monarchies.

...for the Catholic Church Government very much
resembles our constitution, being a limited monarchy,
and hence no form of Church Government, approaches so
nearly to ours as that of the Established Church of
England; the principal difference consisting only in
the difference of the person who governs, and in the
consequences thereof, the one being the successor of
a person constituted in authority by our Saviour, and
the other a person receiving authority from the State
(*CMC*, May 18, 1814. Cf. also, *Works*, V, 91-105).

England used the Gallican theologian Honore Tournelly[22] to show that
the Catholic Church's government had a constitutional balance of
powers in the relationship between the episcopacy and the papacy. According to Tournelly,

The Government of the Church is *not purely* MONARCHICAL
[*sic*] but restrained (temperatum) by an *Aristocracy*;
and the use of the Apostolic power is to be regulated
(moderandus) by the Canons made by the Spirit of God,
and consecrated by the reverence of the whole church.[23]

Both the pope and the bishops were governors in the universal church.
They were two poles of divinely-constituted power and authority. Both
of them, however, were limited powers; they were restricted not only
by the constitution and laws of the church, but also by each other's
authority. In the government of the universal church, according to
England, the pope was not an absolute monarch. England declared
this opinion in an open letter to the national hierarchy:

But as he [pope] is *not* an absolute Monarch, [he]
cannot do those things which only an absolute Monarch
can perform, and hence he concurs with his Fellow
Governors throughout the whole Church, for the
regulation of the general discipline of the entire;
and as the want of his sanction would prevent their
regulations from being valid and binding, so the
want of their concurrence would prevent his mandate
from being obligatory; and here, my Lords, his
superiority of honour and of jurisdiction are

evidently upheld, and yet the principle that they are
Governors, is not only consonant to Faith, but what,
perhaps, under the circumstances of your case is
better, it does not even glance at the long agitated
question of "whether the Pope or the Council be
superior."[24]

England concluded that as the concurrence of the bishops of the world
was necessary for regulating the laws of the universal church, so also
the agreement of the bishops of a particular nation was essential for
formulating the discipline of that nation. Thus, it followed, England
argued, that the national episcopacy, the proper agency for local
discipline within the Catholic Church, had a right to reject papal
demands for the veto. The pope could not change local church
discipline without the local bishops' concurrence. If the bishops rejected such papal demands, they could not thereby be considered
schismatic because "no man can be schismatic for the bare exercise of
his right" (CMC, Aug. 21, 1815).

England saw a very practical reason for denying the pope the right
to change local church discipline. The pope could not understand as
well as territorial bishops the affairs of a particular nation. The
bishops, "whose local knowledge made them the most competent
judges," were the proper persons to decide disciplinary issues in their
particular churches. The pope "whose solicitude for all the churches
made him acquainted with the general state of each" should be most
willing to accept and confirm the bishop's decisions in local matters.
He had to preserve uniformity as far as possible within the universal
church, but the bishops were responsible for accommodating the
general rule and discipline of the church to their special cases (CMC,
March 29, 1816). Even Cardinal Bellarmine, England opined, would
agree to such a position. Bellarmine, England noted, believed that the
pope, previous to his decisions, "ought to consult" the bishops even
though he was not obliged to do so.[25] Bellarmine, of course, was
speaking of papal decisions relating to faith and morals. England applied what Bellarmine said about these matters to local church
discipline. If Bellarmine could see the benefit of papal consultation
before making decisions on faith and morals, he could with even
greater cause perceive the necessity of consulting the bishops in local
church discipline. At any rate, whether or not Bellarmine would agree
to England's adaptation of the principle was of little consequence. The
principle could logically be extended to local discipline.

England also used early ecclesiastical councils, the Church Fathers, theologians and popes to defend the rights of the national church. Provincial churches, he claimed, always had a certain independence from Rome in matters of their own customs, traditions, and special discipline. The decisions of the earliest general councils of the church -- those of the "Council of Ephesus" (431), for example -- supported that position. "It is decreed," England wrote, quoting what he considered an Ephesian canon, "that every Province may preserve pure and inviolate the Rights which it hath of ancient custom."[26] England proceeded to argue that those rights could not be preserved or remain inviolate if the pope could change them when he pleased. Next, England quoted St. Jerome "Who was never suspected of being an enemy of the Holy See." Jerome wrote, in what England believed was Jerome's Fifty-Second Epistle, "Let every Province follow its own Regulations (abundet in suo sensu), and let it consider the Decrees of its Predecessors in the light of Apostolic laws."[27] England continued to argue in light of the conciliar decision and Jerome's testimony that since they had never been repealed nor contradicted, they could be legitimately used in support of the rights of the National Irish Church. Irish Catholics had every reason to believe in their independence as a national church and in their right to determine their own form of episcopal nomination.

After these arguments England concluded with one of his strongest statements on the rights of the episcopacy and, therefore, those of the national church:

> I have very little hesitation in saying, under correction,
> that any interference of his Holiness in the local
> discipline, against the will of the Bishops, is an
> unjust aggression, and an usurpation of power which
> ought to be resisted, and in the present case I am led
> to think it evidently beyond his competency.[28]

England asserted that the claims of the national church were a logical result of defining and limiting papal powers and duties. He believed that the bishops should forcefully and unequivocally declare those rights to the pope during the veto controversy. On August 23, 1815, the national bishops in writing to the pope did assert that he should not and ought not grant the veto because they had not concurred in such a determination; in fact, they had repeatedly opposed it.

The bishops, however, concluded "that the Irish Bishops would cheerfully acquiesce in whatever decision His Holiness would make" (*CMC*, Aug. 22, 1817). England opposed this phrase, calling it Irish "sentiment"; he saw it more as a "matter of compliment than as an acknowledgement of a [papal] right." In a letter to the episcopacy, he asked:

> My Lords, would it not be well in any paper to be
> presented to his Holiness, that such chicanery
> would be guarded against in future, and that your
> Remonstrance should be couched in such language as
> could not bear misinterpretation? (*CMC*, Aug. 30, 1815).

England wanted the national episcopal body to use precise language in acknowledging its own rights and the limits of the papal powers. His concern to restrict authority in the church, moreover, extended to the church councils. He was irate, for example, when rumors were circulated that the British Government had influenced the pope to suspend the Irish bishops for their resistance to the veto; he declared that not even a general council had the power to remove bishops. As the highest authority in the church, it also had constitutional limits which could never be trespassed (*CMC*, Sept. 13, 1815).

England's constitutional view of the church supported his ideological resistance to the veto and confirmed his perception of the rights of the national church by defining the functions of the pope and the bishops. Both were responsible for the government of the universal and the national church, but in different ways. The papacy was the center of Catholic unity; as such the pope had the duty to hold all the national churches in communion, support them and help them to maintain their local identity, call general councils when they were necessary, execute their decisions, and preserve the faith and general discipline of the church throughout the world (*Repertory*, I, 66). The local episcopacy, on the other hand, had the obligation to preserve the communion with the universal church, while accommodating the church as far as possible to the customs, traditions, feelings and political circumstances of the local surroundings.

THE ROLES IN THE NATIONAL CHURCH

The second major question on the church related to the different roles within the national church. Father John Ryan of Dublin was primarily responsible for raising the issue. He had attacked the Irish clergy and laity for their involvement in the veto controversy because they had publicly discussed "spiritual matters" which he felt properly belonged to the domain of the national episcopacy. England and other anti-vetoists, while answering the charge, clarified the roles of bishop, priest and laity within the national church. According to England, the veto question and the changing political and social circumstances had clearly revealed the character of the national church and had brought into focus more sharply than before the diversity of functions within it.

England viewed the national Irish Catholic Church and the different clerical and lay roles in a collegial framework. For him, the national church was the bishops, priests and laity working together for a common end. He repeatedly called for a united effort of the whole church in opposition to the veto:

> Let the Bishops, and the Priests, and the People speak
> out, and speak together, and speak the same language
> ....Let there be but one voice, and one principle of action
> throughout the land, and we must triumph (*CMC*, Aug. 23, 1815).

Within this body, both on the local and on the national level, each of the various members had his own specific function.

England and many of the anti-vetoists viewed the role of the bishop in traditional terms. The bishops, for England, were the official judges in the church. As such, they had the sole responsibility of testing, judging and deciding the value of the testimony they heard. The national episcopal body was the divinely constituted "public tribunal in the church, for ultimate decision" (*Repertory*, II, 507). Before the bishops made their determinations about the laws and direction of the national church, however, they had a responsibility to consult the testimony to the Christian tradition. That tradition, of course, was found in the scriptures, ecclesiastical councils, writings of the church Fathers, papal teachings, and other Christian writings. The clergy and the laity, moreover, were living witnesses to that tradition. It was fitting, therefore, that the bishops, as official representatives and authentic judges of this tradition, listen to the testimony of the clergy and people before announcing local ecclesiastical decisions to the British Government and to the Roman church. Thus, England viewed the bishops primarily as divinely-constituted interpreters and decision makers within the local Christian communities.

England advocated a more active and publicly responsible role for priests and laity in the Catholic Church than was common in Post-Reformation days. As already noted, they were to be living testimonies to the Catholic tradition; as such, they had a public responsibility in the church to preserve and protect that tradition. Wherever it was threatened, as in the veto case, they had the duty to speak out publicly on the issues. England objected to those who charged that priests had no right to bear public testimony in the veto case. He declared that,

> although priests are not *judges* in faith and discipline,
> they may lawfully *discuss* in public *spiritual matters;*
> and they have done so at all times, and will have a
> right to do so in a prudent manner at all times,
> either collectively or individually, provided they are
> always ready, as they ought to be, to submit to the
> decision of the judges, when it shall be made
> (*Repertory*, III, 77; cf. also *CMC*, March 17, 1815).

Before these decisions were made, however, laity and clergy had the right and the obligation to discuss openly matters which concerned their spiritual as well as their temporal welfare. Unlike John Ryan who viewed the veto entirely as an ecclesiastical concern (i.e., it pertained to the exclusive domain of the hierarchy) and unlike Daniel O'Connell who saw it almost exclusively in political terms (i.e., Great Britain sought the veto not for ecclesiastical but for temporal purposes -- to gain more political power over the Irish Catholics), John England perceived it in spiritual (i.e., it involved the freedom of the church) as well as political terms. In mixed questions of this nature, England asserted, the clergy and the laity had a perfect right not only to express themselves publicly but also to participate in the final decisions. In such questions "the ecclesiastical [episcopal] authority is not *exclusively* competent to make a final decision" (*Repertory*, III, 88).

Unlike many of the Irish clergy of his day, England asserted that the clergy in particular must take an active role in political and social issues. England believed that the clergy must sometimes take the initiative and gather together to express themselves publicly, especially in cases where the bishops themselves had refused to act or when they failed to take the lead in defending the rights of the national church and the Irish people (*CMC*, March 17, 1815). He supported clerical involvement in the emancipation movement, moreover, because some of the "more intriguing individuals" in the Irish episcopacy were known to have carried on "underhand negotiations prejudicial to the general good." England attacked Archbishop Thomas Troy of Dublin, in particular, because he believed Troy was at times too easily persuaded by Rome and by the veto arguments.[29] Moreover, England feared that an individual bishop with Troy's prominence in the Irish hierarchy and favor in Rome could use his personal influence to establish ecclesiastical policies that would be harmful to the Irish church. Since individual bishops could misrepresent the national feeling, England believed that the clergy were not only justified, but compelled to "interfere when their interests are affected" (CMC, March 15, 1815). He held that although the priests and the laity were not official judges on the subject of the veto, "yet the public expression of our opinion must necessarily have great weight" (CMC, July 28, 1817).

The priest was not only a witness to the Christian tradition, he was also a political and social reformer. England revealed these roles more through his reform activities than through his intellectual reflections. Because of his participation in the veto question and other political and social reform programs, because of his role in editing a public press, and because of his agitation for the cause of the peasantry, he was severely censured and criticized by many Catholics as well as Protestants. According to his detractors, a priest should not interfere "in secular or political concerns" (Cork Advertiser, Dec. 17, 1818; cf. also, CMC, March 6, Aug. 28, 30, Sept. 2, 1816). England saw his involvement in the veto question as "an indispensable obligation of me, to take a most active part" in the defense of his religion. For him, one could not separate politics and religion in Ireland; they were inextricably united. Numerous denunciations of his activity brought this response: "I am determined if there be any change in my conduct, that it shall be increased activity" (CMC, Sept. 8, 1815).

Bishop Doyle, perhaps more than any other Irish Catholic at the time, gave a theological justification for the priests' political and social reform activities. In 1825, Doyle wrote that the priests' primary role was to proclaim the gospel to the poor. They could not accomplish this task, however, in a social vacuum; they had to identify with the flock in order to announce the gospel (Doyle 1825: 65); they had to know their peoples' conditions and adapt the gospel to their ways. Their mission was necessarily both temporal and spiritual; like Christ, they had to labor as

> advocates of the poor, of the unprotected, and of the
> distressed.... In every nation a clergyman is separated
> from society only that he may labour the more
> efficiently for his fellow-men, and his duty of

administering to their temporal wants is not less pressing
than that of devoting himself to their spiritual
concerns (Doyle 1825: 65; cf. also pp. 312, 314;
McNamee 1969: 49; and MacDonagh 1896: 14).

For Doyle, the Christian tradition demanded that the clergy see the in-
trinsic relationship between the temporal and spiritual affairs of men
and become involved in the social welfare of their country and their
people.

The clerical profession exalts and strengthens the
natural obligation we are all under of labouring for
our country's welfare; and the priests and prophets
of the old law have not only announced and administered
the decrees of heaven but have aided by their counsel
and their conduct the society to which providence
attached them. In the Christian dispensation priests,
and bishops have greatly contributed to the civilization
and improvement of mankind (Doyle 1825: 313).

The spiritual nature and mission of the church did not exclude priests
and bishops from becoming active in temporal affairs; on the contrary,
it was a motivating force behind such participation. Moreover, the
historical circumstances demanded that priests take part in the
political and social reform movements of the day. According to Bishop
Doyle, in Ireland priests had to become involved to help clarify the
political questions which were so closely tied to the theological issues.
In 1826, he noted that the times required "a more extensive acquain-
tance with ecclesiastical matters than those who conduct our political
interests can be well supposed to possess" (Doyle 1826: 11). Thus,
priests were seen to be the spiritual cooperators with the bishop in the
ministry of the gospel in the local church while being at the same time
advocates with the bishops and the laity for the temporal welfare of
their country and their fellowmen.[30]

The middle-class Irish were more active in the church than were
laymen in many other Catholic countries at the time. The theological
justification of their role, however, was not as advanced as their actual
involvement. Even Daniel O'Connell did not seem to have many
developed concepts of the laity's role in the church. He was by no
means priest-ridden; he was submissive to the hierarchy only when he
believed they were preserving the integrity of the Irish church.
Throughout his political life, he felt that the laity had a right to intervene in ecclesiastical affairs when those matters were threatened by

governmental interference or by the acquiescence or "unwisdom" of
the episcopacy (Coldrick 1974: 27).

The functions of the laity in the church, like those of the priest,
provoked much controversy in Ireland. During the veto crisis many of
the bishops were suspicious, to say the least, of the laymen's role in the
questions of the day; many were afraid of "lay control or superintendence" in the church.[31] Many of the lay-initiated conferences,
meetings, dinners and rallies organized in opposition to the veto
frightened some bishops. Some of them feared the development of a
national independence among the laity. Bishop Daniel Delany of
Kildare and Leighlin, for example, did not appreciate lay activism. On
December 30, 1808, he wrote to Bishop Moylan of Cork:

> What Machabee leaders have the People of God nowadays
> got to fight their battles! Ah; My Lord, it is in
> good earnest, high time for *us bishops* at least to adopt
> some other degree of tactics in conducting the spiritual
> warfare in which we are engaged. To the deuce say I for
> one, with these secular manoeuvers. This modern Anglo-Irish
> political system of supporting and extending the
> kingdom of our Divine Master which is not, He tells,
> of this world. Away, away with the politics, with
> committees and their   chairmen, with pamphlet and
> newspaper polemics, with conventions and addresses
> and petitions and the plague knows what applications
> and diplomatic negotiations, at ye seat of Empire,
> with in or out ministers and Professional speechifiers
> in Imperial Parliaments. The *causae majores referendam*,
> as old chronicles tell in days of yore, *ad Curiam Romanam*
> as it lately occurred to me to remark to Dr. Troy in
> writing to his Grace.... Talk of the once boasted Liberties
> of the Gallican Church, forsooth! Pshaw! Give me the
> far more rare privilege of our own little dear Hyberno-
> Anglican Conventical. Vive le Roi! (Bolster 1971: 137).

Delany's sentiments, of course, were not shared by all the bishops of
Ireland, even though they did represent the attitudes of many of the
hierarchy at the time.

John England did not share those apprehensions about the laity. In
fact, he seems to have had a more advanced notion of the role of the
laity than any other cleric or layman in the Irish church at the time. By
their baptism, the laymen belonged to the body of the church and
therefore were entitled to participate in all ecclesiastical decisions not

previously determined by an episcopal body. When Father John Ryan of Dublin opposed lay interference in the veto on the grounds that "mere laymen, with whinning [sic] professions of attachment to Catholic doctrine and to the Prelacy," have actually usurped "the exclusive rights of the episcopacy" (Repertory, III, 85), England raised his voice to defend the laity. He ridiculed Ryan's use of the term "mere laymen" and, as we have already seen, supported the laity's right to participate in the veto question. Their involvement was justified for three reasons: The veto issue was not entirely a spiritual matter and, therefore, not exclusively an episcopal concern. When the laymen began their opposition to the veto, moreover, the spiritual questions in the issue had not yet been decided by the episcopacy. Because the veto involved their own political future, furthermore, the laity had not only a right but a duty to intervene.

Even in matters that were exclusively ecclesiastical, England believed that laymen had a right to express their own opinions. In a meeting of the Cork Aggregate committee on June 8, 1814, the participants discussed the mode that should be used in nominating bishops to vacant sees in Ireland. After a long debate, England and the other participants drew up a number of petitions to be sent to the national hierarchy. In the first resolution, the members declared that all naming to vacant sees should preclude "all foreign and ministerial influence." In addition to this, they declared the mode of proposing they preferred: "and we are certain that the system of Domestic Nomination will give general satisfaction." England suggested an addition to the resolution -- after the words "Domestic Nomination," the words "by Dean and Chapter" should be added. Some laymen at the meeting objected that the "laity are not justified in intervening in Ecclesiastical matters." England responded by saying that the bishops have the right to decide on these affairs, but the laity were at "perfect liberty" to make suggestions until the issue was settled by an episcopal decision (CMC, June 8, 1814). England's experiences with the power of public opinion in politics seem to have influenced his view of the laymen's right to be heard in matters solely concerned with ecclesiastical affairs. He was not really being innovative; he was simply taking advantage of the existing freedom within the church. Where nothing had been declared by an authoritative decision, he felt completely free to express himself; he also asserted that those same liberties were open to the laity. His theological perception of the laity perhaps differed very little from that of his contemporaries, but his experiences with them had in fact given him a new vision of their role within the church.

England's involvement with the laity of Cork in opposition to the veto question and in the politico-religious struggle for unqualified emancipation gave him a democratic conception of the laity within the church which manifested itself in Ireland in his support of their rights in the church. It was also, perhaps, this experience which helped him support the cause of the laity in the United States.

CHAPTER V

john england's irish experience

By 1820, England's intellectual formation as well as his political and ecclesiastical experiences had prepared him in three major ways for many of the political and religious realities and ideologies he would encounter in the United States. First, because of their own political and religious environment, John England and his colleagues saw the shifting conditions in the world as advantageous to the Catholic Church; the Irish church, at least, had gained greater freedom from the revolutions and the transitional times. England and his fellow-liberals, therefore, were accustomed to speaking of change, reform, adaptation, republicanism, and democracy as beneficial to the Catholic Church. Although elements in the contemporary world were inimical to the Catholic Church, they were seen as extrinsic entities within a world generally full of opportunity, freedom, growth, and promise. England had confidence in the future. This explains, in part, why he differed from the more conservative Irish bishops, felt at home with the liberal Irish laity, and developed an openness to the possibilities of democracy within the church in the United States.

Secondly, John England and his associates had formulated ideological positions which were consistent with those held by most in the American community. The political and religious events had

stimulated England and his friends to examine the records of the
Christian experience in order to discover the message which would en-
lighten their contemporary experiences, justify their desire to preserve
their Irish Catholic tradition, and give a Christian ideological foundation for their hopes for future changes in their civil and religious
conditions. In the search, England, in particular, began to read the
scriptures, the church Fathers, theologians and canon law in light of
his political experiences and principles, and began to formulate liberal
views of the separation of church and state, voluntaryism, and
religious and civil liberty. His formulation of these positions was influenced by the Irish experience and intensified by people like Arthur
O'Leary, Daniel O'Connell and other leading Irish thinkers of the day.
Although it may have been partially motivated by the long-established
hostility for the British Government, England's development of an
ideological basis for the separation of church and state and the voluntary nature of religion was primarily an attempt to preserve Irish
traditions. The formation of a Catholic position on religious freedom
was an effort to justify the movement for a change in the Irish
Catholics' civil and religious circumstances; but it was also an ar-
ticulation of principle. Although the development of ideological principles on these subjects was historically conditioned, the truths themselves were accepted as intrinsically human and Christian. Even
though John England and many of his mentality did not perceive these
principles as absolutely applicable in every historical circumstance,
they did see them as ideals to be realized wherever practically possible.

Thirdly, and more specifically, John England's ecclesiastical experiences and his theological conception of the Catholic Church also
prepared him for American Catholic life. England's political experiences and ideology influenced the way he viewed the ecclesiastical community. For him, the church, like the political community, was based
upon a constitution. The entire church was divided into various
segments; each part had its own constitutional freedoms and responsibilities; and each was spiritually and constitutionally united to the
universal communion. Because of this constitutional view and because
of his Irish Nationalism, England believed in a strong local church
which had laws, customs and characteristics peculiar to the national
political and social circumstances. Like the political community,
moreover, the church had its own constitutional description of the
roles, duties and rights of all its members. More specifically, the church
was like a court of law in which the bishops, like judges, were the

ultimate source of decision; the witnesses were the scriptures, the tradition, church laws and the living testimony of the priests and people. The church, therefore, was the entire people working together for a common end -- on the temporal as well as the spiritual level of human life. Thus, England's democratic experiences in the political reform movements and his constitutional view of ecclesiastical powers and duties blended to produce a collegial understanding of the church.

SECTION III

---

american republicanism

In Cork, on September 21, 1820, John England was consecrated bishop of the newly-erected Diocese of Charleston which included the three states of South Carolina, North Carolina, and Georgia.[1] The thirty-four-year-old immigrant bishop arrived in the new diocese on December 30, 1820. From 1820 until his death in 1842, he encountered two significant problems tormenting American Catholicism: nativism (see Billington 1964) and trusteeism (see Guilday 1927: I, 124-282; Carey 1975: 140-268; Carey 1976: 85-98). On the one hand, the American nativists were attacking Catholicism from the outside, charging that it was foreign to and incompatible with Americanism -- especially with some of its unique features: religious liberty, separation of church and state, voluntaryism, and republicanism. On the other hand, the Catholic trustees, who were the laity and clergy legally responsible for the temporal administration of the local congregations, were demanding from within Catholicism greater lay and clerical participation in ecclesiastical decision-making. They also insisted that the church appropriate more democratic procedures in its own internal operations. In a way, they were seeking to reform the Catholic Church by identifying it with the principles and practices of American republicanism. Like the nativists, they found the current American disposition of Catholicism inconsistent with republicanism. Thus, the Catholic trustees as well as the American nativists raised the single, most important practical and ideological question for American Catholicism throughout the nineteenth century: what was the precise relationship between Catholicism and the unique features of American republicanism?

While responding to the nativists and trustees as well as to the issue they raised, England became the most visible and articulate clerical spokesman for a liberal and constitutional American Catholic tradition. He addressed numerous tracts to the nativists, illuminating what he considered the Catholic position on the charges of the day. In reply to the trustees, he created a constitutional form of diocesan government which incorporated elements of republicanism while preserving the Catholic structures of episcopal government. The influence of his Irish background shows through repeatedly in his apology for Catholicism in its American setting. How American circumstances conditioned his theology of the church is also transparent in his writings and in his attempts to accomodate Irish Catholicism to the American way of life.

England's American apologetical writings[2] reveal his concept of the relationship between the unique principles of American republicanism and Catholic thought. His constitutional form of diocesan government analyzed within the context of his apologetics discloses his ideas on accommodation and his perception of the republicanism inherent in Catholic principles and practices.

John England believed that Catholicism was essentially compatible with the unique features of American republicanism. The American Constitution, in England's estimation, was "essentially different" from any other existing political constitution because it was based upon religious liberty and the separation of church and state (*Works*, IV, 53); the practice of voluntaryism in the churches was another beneficial characteristic in American republicanism. According to England, these ideas and practices were not, as some people believed, antithetical to those of the Catholic Church; rather, they were part of a Catholic heritage.

CHAPTER I

---

religious liberty

England believed that when he came to America he did not have to change his religious or political principles.

> I profess in America what I professed in Ireland, and
> what they who were my associates in Ireland still
> profess. I may indeed say with truth of myself, what
> was said not exactly in the same meaning of others,
> Coelum, non animum mutant, qui trans mare current.
> I have not in America changed nor dissembled a single
> principle, either political or religious, which I have
> cherished (*Works*, V, 148).

In fact, he felt that the Irish adapted to the American political and religious experiences more easily than other immigrant groups because of their former experiences in Ireland.

> The Irish are easily amalgamated with the Americans.
> Their principles, their dispositions, their politics,
> their notion of government, their language and their
> appearance become American very quickly, and they
> praise and prefer America to their oppressors at home
> (Guilday 1927: I, 481-82, quoting England to
> Dr. Michael O'Connor, February 25, 1835).

In the United States, as in Ireland, therefore, England forcefully advocated the principle of religious liberty. The words "civil and religious freedom" were rallying calls for the Irish as well as the Americans during this period of history (1820 to 1842). For the Irish in America the words were doubly meaningful. They referred to their American experiences and they expressed their hopes for the emancipation of Catholics in Ireland. In the United States, as in Ireland, numerous movements were sympathetic to the drive for civil and religious freedom throughout the world. When the Irish, and John England in particular, came to the United States, they readily joined their American neighbors in supporting these campaigns.

The Irish experiences of civil and religious liberty nevertheless, differed from those in America. For the most part, these freedoms were a legal reality in the United States, whereas they were only a hope in Ireland. Although some states still retained statutes against Catholics and Jews, legal intolerance in America was not the most significant problem for Irish Catholics. In Ireland Catholics were in the majority; in the United States they were a tiny minority in the 1820's. As a minority, they encountered religious toleration in the federal and in most state constitutions, but they did not find a corresponding tolerance in the hearts of the American people. One of England's chief tasks, therefore, was to expose and to suggest ways to eradicate the sources of intolerance. American religious pluralism also forced England to consider religious liberty in a context which had little similarity to his Irish background. In the process of responding to these different American conditions, England developed more fully his ideas on religious liberty.

According to England, civil liberty was "the enjoyment of equal Rights and Privileges, the Liberty of doing everything not forbidden by law." Religious liberty meant "the right of every man to follow the dictates of his conscience in the belief of doctrines purely religious without being subject, on that account, to civil pains and disabilities" (*USCM*, Jan. 27, 1827: 212). He denied nativists' charges that Catholics believed the church had the authority to inflict bodily pain upon men for errors of faith. No church and no state had such power from God.

> My belief is that God never gave to any Pope, nor to
> any other Bishop, nor to any other clergyman, nor to
> any state, nor to any human tribunal, any power,
> directly or indirectly, to inflict any corporal or
> temporal punishment upon man for heresy or religious
> error (*Works*, II, 256; cf. II, 468).

For England, the rights of a man's personal conscience were inalienable. No external force could require a man to profess what he did not believe, nor compel him to entertain any particular speculative opinions; the prerogatives of conscience were supreme (*Works*, I, 177; cf. III, 61; IV, 54). Even though Catholics and Protestants had been religious persecutors in the past, Catholic tenets had neither condoned nor supported such abuses (*Works*, III, 96-97). Whether legal or otherwise, persecution for religious belief was never Christian (*Works*, III, 89, 91).

England and other American Catholics had to face the fact that their beliefs on religious liberty were not consistent with current papal teachings. American Protestants were justly apprehensive about Catholic professions of religious freedom because of papal teachings like Gregory XVI's *Mirari Vos* of August 15, 1832. John Breckenridge, a Presbyterian minister in Philadelphia, and other Protestants used the encyclical against American Catholics; it proved, they thought, that Catholics were opposed to religious liberty in principle and that in the United States they were only putting up with it until they could gain control of the country (Hughes 1836: 300).

Mirari Vos called "liberty of conscience" an absurd and erroneous doctrine which had its pernicious origins in an attitude of religious indifference. Thus, the encyclical condemned those who considered the doctrine advantageous to the church in a new democratic and pluralistic age. Gregory XVI maintained that the "most prolific cause" of the evils of the church was the "depraved principle" of religious indifference. That principle held that eternal salvation was equally attainable in any profession of faith, provided the natural dictates of morality were observed. The papal teaching asserted, moreover, that Christians would "without doubt perish eternally, unless they hold fast the Catholic faith, and preserve it whole and inviolate."[3]

American Catholic responses to *Mirari Vos* and to nativist Protestant charges regarding the encyclical were unconvincing, to say the least. Catholics like the cleric John Hughes of Philadelphia denied that the Catholic Church denounced religious liberty and liberty of conscience. The encyclical, he held, condemned only the abuses of sound principles (Hughes 1836: 51, 77, 79, 369). The encyclical, however, saw the principles themselves, not simply their abuse, as the source of the evils of the day. England, unlike Hughes, never really dealt with the encyclical when he defended Catholic teaching. As already noted, he believed that the papacy was not the sole organ in the church for defining church doctrine. (This belief may have been partly responsible for his inattention to the papal letter.) He also may have been simply embarrassed that his position clashed with that of the pope's.

Or, because of his various trips to Rome and his conversations with Gregory XVI, perhaps he realized that Rome recognized the great difference between European and American circumstances in regard to contemporary liberal movements (See Hales 1960: 281). What had been destructive to the church in Europe, was advantageous to the church in Ireland and in the United States. Whatever his reason, England neither defended the papal letter nor did he try to explain the differences between his own position and that of the pope. He simply reasserted his own "Catholic" position -- even though it contradicted papal teaching. Thus, American Catholic inadequacy in response to the encyclical tended to intensify Protestant suspicions.

Unlike Gregory XVI, England did not equate religious liberty and freedom of conscience with religious indifference[4]; nor did he hold an exclusivist view of salvation. Living in a pluralistic religious community, England constantly told Catholics that the Christian was by nature a liberal person in that he was called to love all persons, to hold fast to his own beliefs, to judge no one to be in error in matters of religious belief and to "leave the final judgment always to God."

> I cannot say to him [who differs from me in matters
> of religion], "I know that what you profess is not true"
> -- but I may say -- I have no doubt that what the Saviour
> taught is what I believe, but I know not the lights you
> may have had, God does." (Works, IV, 229).

Christian charity demanded that the individual Christian seek truth, allow others to pursue it in their own way, and condemn no person who honestly differed from oneself in his religious opinions. The Christian who lived in a religiously diverse community was reminded of the gospel parable of the tares and the wheat.

> This is the case, in which an enemy has sown tares
> through the wheat; both spring up together: and yet
> the Saviour declares that we must leave the time of
> separation to his own harvest, when, in the order of
> nature, death will have cut down both (Works, IV, 55).

The Christian preserved truth, charity and religious toleration, and at the same time left God and conscience the ultimate right of judging the final results of a man's beliefs and practices (Works, II, 352-53; IV, 190; V, 55). Men were honestly mistaken at times about religious doctrines; but, they could still be saved if they responded to God's grace and lived in compliance with His "voluntary covenant" (USCM, April 30, 1831: 350).

According to England, religious toleration and religious liberty meant more than just the legal recognition of the rights of others to believe and worship according to their own consciences. During the hostile days of the "Protestant Crusade," the definition of religious toleration had to be extended beyond its legal limits.

> Equal religious rights does [sic] not consist in a mere
> permission to worship God according to the dictates of
> one's conscience; it consists in the security of the
> feelings from insult, and the protection of the citizen from
> the contumely of the self-sufficient, the arrogant, or the
> uninformed; equally as in eligibility to office
> (USCM, Dec. 26, 1829: 206).

Intolerance of Catholics in America, according to England, had several major causes. Once those reasons were recognized by the Catholic community, that prejudice would be more easily understood and effective remedies could be applied to lessen the bigotry and bring about a more amiable atmosphere in the relationships between the various religions in the United States. Religious bias had its primary source not in bad feelings about Catholics, but in English-influenced education, especially the English view of Catholics in history. Catholic tenets and character were misrepresented in the texts used in American schools. Histories, science books, and even the *belles lettres* had incorrectly presented Catholics to their American readers. Family ties also strengthened prejudices against Catholics. People naturally believed what they had been told at home by their parents, and early biases were not easily overcome. Religious feelings also produced intolerance against Catholics; people felt that their own religious foundations were superior to those of others. To extricate a people from the feelings and beliefs engendered for centuries by their religious institutions was most difficult. For an American Protestant "to be free from violent prejudice against Catholics" was, therefore almost impossible. Catholics, however, had the primary responsibility to correct this bigotry. "We should rather endeavor by proper means to remove it, than blame those who are its victims, because they cannot do what is impossible."[5] According to England, the solution to the problem of intolerance lay in a Catholic elucidation of history and Catholic tenets.[6] Rather than being vindictive, the exposition was intended to explain Catholic tenets and practices which had been misunderstood.

England's belief that true Christian liberality should eliminate all prejudices and all civil laws against any religious denomination, led him to support the rights of all groups in the United States and in the world who were seeking emancipation from civil disabilities for their religious opinions. In 1825, England wrote an open letter to Daniel O'Connell indicating the practical consequences of the principle of universal religious freedom:

> The principle is that of the great, good venerable,
> liberal and charitable Protestant Bishop of Norwich.
> A principle which, as you have frequently expressed
> yourself, would give emancipation to the Catholic in
> Great Britain (let me add in North Carolina and New
> Jersey), to the Protestant in Spain, and to the Christian
> in Constantinople (*USCM*, July 13, 1825: 19).

At different times during his ministry in Charleston, England led or participated in movements to promote the rights of all religious denominations. The diminution of the civil liberties of any one particular religious group, he believed, would eventually lead to the destruction of the rights of all (*USCM*, July 8, 1837: 14). He sought to have the civil disabilities removed from the laws of North Carolina and New Jersey in regard to Catholics, and in Maryland in regard to Jews (*USCM*, July 18, 1835: 22; cf. also *Works*, I, 16). He joined a number of committees in Charleston at various times during his ministry to petition various countries for the emancipation of different religious denominations, or to protest the persecution of a particular sect. He preached charity sermons in order to collect funds for the freedom of the Greeks (*USCM*, Feb. 4, 1824: 76; Feb. 18, 1824: 100-105); he joined with the Protestant citizens of Charleston to call for the emancipation of Irish Catholics (*USCM*, Sept. 27, 1828: 89). He likewise supported freedom for the Jews in England, Bavaria, Damascus and Rhodes, and joined committees in Charleston to promote those causes in the United States.[7]

CHAPTER II

---

separation of church and state

Although England acknowledged that the Catholic Church had no doctrine on the precise relationship between the church and the state, he himself advocated the separation of the two. His American experiences confirmed and strengthened his former Irish position. In Ireland he saw separation as an historical ideal; in the United States, however, he promoted the idea as *the* ideal relationship between the two. Because of his American position, he has been called "the first theoretician in the American Catholic Church on Church-State questions."[8]

In his diocesan constitution, where he outlined essential doctrines, England stated as Catholic belief that "Church government and temporal government are not necessarily united the one to the other, nor dependent the one upon the other" (*Works*, V, 95). Jesus Christ did not grant the state power over spiritual or ecclesiastical concerns; nor did he give the church authority over secular governments. In one of his apological writings England reaffirmed this point.

> It is heresy in religion; it is an absurdity in politics to
> assert, that because a man possesses political power there
> he possesses ecclesiastical jurisdiction: or that because he
> has spiritual power, he therefore has magisterial rights in

the state. The doctrine of the Roman Catholic Church
and the principles of the American Constitution are in
unison upon this subject (*Works*, II, 249).

When nativists charged Catholics with accepting the proposition
"that the civil power ought to be united with the ecclesiastical,"
England responded that the position "is totally false, and so far from
being Catholic doctrine [that it] has something of the appearance of
heresy, though not absolutely heretical" (*Works* II, 289). In the first
ages of Christianity, political and ecclesiastical powers were separated.
Any other relationship was dangerous.

When nativists also accused Catholics of maintaining that the pope is
not only a spiritual pastor but also a temporal prince, England replied
that the proposition was true only when it was not connected with any
doctrine about the church's relationship to state powers. The assertion
was an historical fact, but it was not a specific Catholic doctrine
(*Works*, II, 289).

As in Ireland, so also in the United States, England opposed beliefs
which he though were falsely attributed to Catholicism. He argued
against the position taken by Bellarmine on the pope's indirect power
in temporal affairs (*Works*, II, 235). He affirmed, moreover, that
Catholics had no divided allegiance, the one to the church (as a foreign
power) and the other to the American state (*Works*, II, 483). According to England, Catholics believed that political power was derived
directly from the people and spiritual power came only from God
(*Works*, II, 250-51). As they were separated in their sources, so also
they should be separated in their exercise. The union of church and
state had enslaved the church in the past and had given too much
power to the political governments over the liberties of the people
(*Works*, III, 291; V, 56). The safest and most natural relationship between the two, therefore, was that of separation.

> There never was a union of church and state which did
> not bring serious evils to religion;... But I do know that
> the Founder of our faith did not unite the church and
> state;... Without writing harshly of thousands of good and
> better men who differ from me in opinion, I am
> convinced that a total separation from the temporal
> government, is the most natural and safest state for the
> church in any place where it is not, as in the papal
> territory, a complete government of churchmen.[9]

In the 1830's, when Félicité de Lamennais was calling for a separation of the church and state in France, England supported that position in his *Miscellany* (*USCM*, Dec. 11, 1830: 190; Jan. 15, 1831: 230-31; Jan. 22, 1831: 238-39; March 19, 1831: 303). When he was accused of interfering in foreign ecclesiastical affairs which he had no competence to judge, England replied that he would discontinue his comments upon the French Church, but he could not refrain from declaring,

> Yet we must in expressing our wish that the church may
> not continue an appendage to the state, not be considered
> as censuring the prelates, should they, who are the best
> judges of their own circumstances, perceive that as yet
> there exists what we must call an unfortunate necessity
> therefore (*USCM*, Jan. 22, 1831: 238).

When Lamennais or at least his opinions were condemned in Gregory XVI's encyclical *Mirari Vos*, England was in Rome on a mission for his diocese. The encyclical upheld the union of church and state and practically denounced the separation of the two. The encyclical also contradicted England's position on the historical effects of church-state unions. England held that such unions produced evils for both the church and state. The pope declared, "that this union is dreaded by the profane lovers of liberty, only because it has never failed to confer prosperity on both" (*USCM*, June 7, 1834: 385-86). The papal letter was not published in the *Miscellany* until almost two years after its promulgation, and then it was printed only because it had appeared in other papers hostile to Catholicism. A diocesan priest who assumed editorship of the *Miscellany* while England returned to Rome, was obviously embarrassed by the papal teaching. Excusing himself for waiting almost two years before publishing the document, the editor noted,

> We would in a particular manner invite the attention of
> the laity to this interesting letter, as some of our *fanatical*
> prints have not neglected to garble and misrepresent it, with
> a degree of bigotry peculiar to themselves; and sure it might
> be expected, that our neighbor, the *Observer*, would be
> foremost amongst the first of our slanderers.[10]

The nativists perceived the obvious contradiction between the American and Roman positions and repeatedly pointed to the differences, holding that the "true" Catholic position was found in the "infallible" Roman rather than in the fallible American assertions (See e.g., Hughes 1836: 42-43; 104; 301f.; 338). For obvious reasons, American Catholics failed to deny the papal teachings and, as in the case of religious liberty, this widened the gap between nativists and themselves. To the nativists, American Catholics' assertions of their own Catholicism remained credible, but their professions of Americanism continued to be unbelievable.

England neither defended the encyclical nor did he try to reconcile it with his own teaching. The papal letter, however, did not stop him from advocating his former positions. After 1834, i.e., after the publication of the encyclical and after his return from Rome, he continued to support the principle and the historical necessity of separation. In 1836, for example, he wrote,

> I do not know any system more favorable to the security
> of religious rights and of church property than that of the
> American law.... I prefer it to the law of almost every Catholic
> country with which I am acquainted (*Works*, II, 241).

Constitutional separation had a number of logical and practical consequences. According to England, the Christian's life was divided into two distinct parts (as separate as church and state): the life of the citizen and that of the believer (*Works*, IV, 303-14). As a citizen, one's life was directed toward temporal and political goods; as a believer, one was committed to strive toward eternal, spiritual happiness. The citizen was responsible for the state and his own temporal welfare, while the believer was accountable for the church and his own sanctification. For England, this division of life was most clearly expressed in the Christian leader's responsibilities in a country where church and state were legally separated. The leader was responsible for a man's salvation (*Works*, IV, 208); he had no reason or right to interfere in political concerns in the United States (*Works*, V, 144-45). His only obligation was to support the state and the common decisions of society. This duty was based upon the reciprocal relationship between religion and society. Whatever affected the one affected the other.

> War is not only calamitous in its effects upon society,
> but is injurious to religion by destroying charity and
> by exciting passions. For the same reason, the
> maladministration of government, by those to whom it
> has been committed, is injurious to religion because it
> produces innumerable evils, and excites the worst
> passions (*Works*, IV, 280).

Hence, it followed that the religious leader had the mandate to in-
culcate the general Christian principles of love and brotherhood in order to support a stable society and thereby secure good civil leadership
(*Works*, IV, 304). For England, Christian charity was the basis of good
citizenship and patriotism. Thus, the church was not totally removed
from the political life of the people; in fact, it was the primary support
of the state, patriotism and all legal authority (*Works*, IV, 228).

The church's authority, however, was restricted as a consequence of
separation. The church's only power was spiritual persuasion.
Although it had the power to make rules, regulations, statutes and censures for its own internal discipline, it had no political or temporal
authority to enforce them. The church was a voluntary society and individuals could either accept the consequences of membership in such a
community or they were free to leave.

The idea of separation also limited the state's powers. The state had
no authority, for example, to restrict the sending of mail on Sundays
because of religious reasons or because of pressure from religious
groups; nor did it have a right to legislate in areas of personal morality,
e.g., prohibiting the use of whiskey on Sundays or adding taxes to
whiskey for the purpose of giving revenue to religious missionaries
(*Works*, IV, 49). The state also had no power to interfere in the internal discipline of any church, as some had requested (*Works*, V, 214-16;
227). During the years of England's ministry in the United States, the
full legal implications of the constitutional separation were not yet
realized; England found it necessary, therefore, to reject state interference in what he thought were purely spiritual or ecclesiastical matters.

CHAPTER III

voluntaryism

England's belief in religious liberty and in the separation of church and state came out of an Irish experience which, as already noted, led him to refer to the church as a "voluntary covenant." For England, as for most Irish Catholic immigrants, American voluntaryism presented no obstacles to assimilation. Their Irish experiences for centuries had prepared them for it.[11] Thus, in the United States, England continued to advocate the principle and practice of voluntaryism. The church was legally-free in the United States; it suffered no external temporal restraints nor could it use the power of the state to enforce its own rules and regulations. It had to rely solely upon spiritual persuasion to enforce ecclesiastical discipline and upon the voluntary contributions of its membership for its financial support.

Because of the American legal circumstances and the troubles which occurred during the trustee controversies, England was forced to consider the principle of voluntaryism on two different levels. On the one hand, he continued to fight against all state aid of religion because such support always implied a certain control and jeopardized the freedom of the church. On the other hand, he had to combat exclusive lay control of financial contributions because such control generally destroyed the freedom of the clergy and the gospel within the church. For him, the principle of voluntaryism meant that the church and the clergy had to be free from lay dominance as well as state influence.

England fought against state aid of religion for some of the same reasons he had opposed it in Ireland. He believed that whenever the state supported the church, the church lived in a certain degree of wealth and comfort. This almost always distracted the clergy from their proper religious vocations and sometimes made them pawns of the state (*Works*, I, 438; cf. also III, 512). He preferred, therefore, "infinitely more, church liberty and poverty to this subjugation accompanied by the most splendid endowments" (Papers Relating 1897: 303, 306). In Ireland, for example, when the Presbyterian clergy were given state support they lost their freedom and became appendages of the British government.[12] The Irish Catholic priests, however, like the clergy in the primitive church, lived in poverty believing that "their kingdom was not of this world."[13] Because of this and because they depended upon the voluntary gifts of the laity to sustain them, they kept the church free and independent. Voluntary support, therefore, was the principal means of the liberty of the church (*USCM*, Jan. 15, 1831: 230-231; Jan. 31, 1832: 236).

England also believed that many American Catholic trustees had endangered ecclesiastical liberty. Although he did not reject the trustee system itself, he did vigorously oppose its excesses. He felt that whoever controlled the purse controlled the pastor. The trustees' particular system of financial administration required "from the clergyman concessions incompatible with his duty, and reduced him to the alternative of betraying his conscience, or forfeiting the means of his support" (*Diurnal*, 203-04). England, therefore, opposed such a system with as much vigor as he had the veto and the union of church and state. He felt that the trustees' financing could tempt the Catholic clergy to give up their evangelical freedom for ease and comfort of life. He resisted trusteeism, moreover, because it produced "the curse of an oligarchical tyranny of the worst description" (Papers Relating 1897: 312). He censured the trustees, furthermore, because they had created a means of obtaining funds for the support of the church which was altogether inimical to the gospel. England vehemently opposed the trustee practice of renting out pews to members of the parish in order to support the church because,

> By their means a very painful and galling distinction is created between the rich and poor which causes pride and conceit in the one, and mortification and shame in the other, where both ought to be on a footing of equality before their common maker (*Diurnal*, 302).

Voluntaryism should provide all with equal access to the church and the benefits of religion. The peculiar trustee practice of collecting pew rents, therefore, was incompatible with the purpose of voluntaryism. When England dedicated the first new church in Charleston, he wrote in the *Miscellany*,

> There are no pews nor private seats in the church which
> has been erected, nor is it intended there should be, for
> it is conceived by its superintendents that the house of God
> should be open to all, and that the benefits of religion should
> not be confined to a few purchasers and sold like the goods
> of this world; but that the poor should have equal opportunities
> of being instructed as the rich -- there are convenient benches
> which are equally free to persons of all persuasions -- no
> member of the congregation having a right of precedence
> to any other well conducted person who may be present
> (*USCM*, June 5, 1822: 5).

In his diocesan constitution, which will be analyzed more fully elsewhere in this section, England not only revealed his acceptance of vountaryism but also showed that its practice had to be limited by specific regulations. Thus, he established controls upon the trustees' particular management of voluntary offerings. The constitution set limits upon the lay trustees' collection and distribution of voluntary support so that the clergy's freedom would be maintained and the laity's right to have an effective voice through their voluntary contributions would also be upheld. Only in this way could a good relationship be maintained between the clergy and the people; through his system the clergy were still dependent upon the laity's voluntary offerings for their maintenance, but they were not controlled by them in the exercise of their ministerial functions. He believed the relationship between the pastor and his people should be one of friendship and that the voluntary system of support could "cement this affection."

> A pastor who feels himself to a certain extent dependent
> upon the good will of his flock, will be frequently urged
> to reflect upon the best mode of securing their
> affection, for it is his interest. He is not the slave
> of any individual nor of any faction, though he must
> endeavor to conciliate all (Papers Relating 1897: 307).

According to England, the principle of voluntaryism within the context of American legal thought implied not only the free-will financial support of the church, but also the liberty to form voluntary associations. The constitution which he established for his own diocese implemented this principle. The constitution created various corporations for the management of parish and diocesan ecclesiastical affairs thereby acknowledging that religious congregations could not be "legally held without their voluntary acceptance" (Papers Relating 1897: 317). The constitution used the American laws to bind Catholics together in a legal and moral union. In 1836, England reported to the Society for the Propagation of the Faith in France that the nature of American law was particularly valuable because it allowed the church a maximum amount of freedom in establishing its own constitutional basis for government.

> In a word, they [Catholics] can voluntarily bind
> themselves by special acts to maintain and observe
> the whole doctrine and discipline of their church,
> and can regulate that no person shall be admitted
> a member of their association without his undertaking
> this obligation, or shall continue a member if he violates
> his contract for such observance (*Works*, III, 241-42).

England realized that by including these elements in the constitution and by listing the requirements of persons for belonging to the church he was following the provisions of American laws regarding voluntary associations.

As the American laws recognized the perfect freedom of all individuals to join their own voluntary corporations, so the diocesan constitution acknowledged the freedom of all Catholics to accept or reject its provisions. No parish, no priest, no layman had to consent to the constitution. If Catholics did not choose willingly to approve it, they were not be cut off from Catholic communion. In fact, England noted, "they shall have our good wishes, our friendly offices and our religious intercourse" (*Works*, V, 421). He realized that all Catholics did not accept every constitutional provision. Some refused to approve the document because they could not agree with the regulations for managing ecclesiastical temporalities. They were left free to dissent (*USCM*, Jan. 28, 1824: 59-60). When the last church, St. Mary's of Charleston, confirmed the constitution in 1830, England simply acknowledged its presence in the yearly convention saying: "Blessed be God! We have amongst us the most perfect harmony and the most cordial union" (*Works*, V, 425).

Even those laity and clergy who accepted all the provisions of the document and participated each year in the constitutionally-established diocesan conventions were perfectly free to express themselves openly on all matters of diocesan welfare. England realized that the constitutional system was imperfect; throughout the course of the yearly conventions he was open to revisions in the changeable parts of the constitution (*Works*, IV, 421-22). Periodically, he asked the convention delegates to suggest useful modifications in the constitution in order to bring about a more effective administration in the diocese (*Works*, IV, 334). From the beginning of the formation of the constitution, he had consulted a number of lawyers, especially William Gaston, on the legal provisions of the document (*Diurnal*, 222). At the first meeting of Catholics in North Carolina, the assembly accepted, with England's concurrence, a number of amendments suggested by Gaston and others (*USCM*, Feb. 25, 1824: 128). From the first conventions until the last, England left the priests and lay delegates free to decide necessary changes or additions (*USCM*, March 24, 1824: 191-92). Only free expression and voluntary acceptance could assure an enthusiastic support for the system of government. The lay and clerical resolutions after each convention revealed a hearty approval of the system and a willing collaboration in its measures. On July 7, 1832, for example, the diocesan clergy and laity published an enthusiastic statement supporting the constitution and convention system and acknowledging England's leadership in the diocesan church.

> Inadequate indeed is the power of words to describe
> the gratitude and affection, which the discharge of
> your duties as a prelate and a friend has deeply
> fixed in the hearts of all your flock.... There
> is a more solemn voice which comes from the embodied
> spirit of thousands; it is the voice of your church
> -- of your people. For them you have accomplished
> that for which they must be ever thankful (*USCM*,
> July 7, 1832: 222).

The high priority Americans put on freedom influenced England not only in the construction of his constitution, but also in his frequent explanations of the nature of liberty within the Catholic Church. England asserted that prelates in the church generally sought the advice and opinions of the clergy and laity on matters relating to their welfare. At times the clergy and laity disagreed with their bishops; but, there "is ample scope for difference of opinion" as long as defined doctrines of the church were neither denied nor contradicted. In the area of church discipline,

we are at liberty respectfully to give our opinion
regarding the expediency or inexpediency of the law,
the utility or the inaptitude of the discipline. We have
therefore all that liberty which is consistent with
good sense, good order, and the general good. We have
just as much as any citizen has in any well organized
state. It is true that we believe the Constitution of
the Church cannot be changed; because it emanates from
God and not from man:... but the legislation of the
church is so far liable to change, as that it may by
proper tribunals be accommodated to the circumstances
of time and place not only to preserve order but to
promote the purity and the prosperity of the body of
the faithful (*Works*, I, 435-36).

For England, the church in this country should emphasize those
elements of the American experience, like freedom, which would
"promote the purity and the prosperity of the body of the faithful."

The church was free not only to adapt its legislation and discipline to
different circumstances, but also to entertain a variety of religious
opinions. Some Protestants had charged that Catholicism prevented
free inquiry because it taught that church doctrines were unchanging.
England replied: Where God did not teach, Christians were at perfect
liberty to form their own opinions (*Works*, II, 81; I, 166). England,
nevertheless, reminded Catholics that religion was not a matter of
opinion, but in fact: freedom was allowed for inquiry where the fact of
revelation had not been decided (*USCM*, Feb. 4, 1824:66). A great
diversity of speculation was possible in areas of revelation not
dogmatically defined by the church (*Works*, III, 454). Even in church
councils, where matters of doctrine were to be defined, bishops had the
maximum amount of freedom to investigate the evidence and to express
their views about their findings. Through such free inquiry and expression of opinion, truth could be reached (*Works*, II, 82; cf. also
O'Shea 1904: 224).

The American experience, of course, helped England bring out those
elements in the Catholic tradition which stressed freedom *within* the
church. He may also have been assisted in this regard by one of his·
favorite French authors, Chateaubriand. Like Chateaubriand
(Chateaubriand 1856: 48-49), England emphasized not only freedom,
but also representation, consultation, democracy, diversity and dissent
within the Catholic tradition.

Although England stressed Christian liberty, he also pointed out the
limits of that freedom. Liberty within the church did not mean license

nor did it imply that man was freed from the responsibility to search
for the truth. Freedom within the church, in fact, was limited not only
by god's revelation but also by ecclesiastical authority. Although all
men had a natural and God-given right to liberty of conscience and independence of thought, they were not entirely free to believe whatever
they pleased concerning religion and God. Since it was a principle of
natural reason that a man had no right to reject truth and to choose
error, it followed that men had no right of choice respecting the tenets
of religion that God had revealed (*Works*, I, 183-4). Religious freedor
meant that a man was emancipated from all external restraints coi
cerning his beliefs; but Christian voluntaryism meant something ei
tirely different:

> Christian liberty properly understood means that man is
> free where God has not bound him; but where God
> declares what is his will, man is no longer free, he is
> at that moment bound to believe; knowledge is a blessing;
> faith is a privilege, it is the communication of heavenly
> wisdom, man should receive it as his best good, as the dearest
> pledge of his teacher's affection (*Works*, I, 249).

God's revelation was a matter of certitude. Men could discover the
truth of God's will by submitting to the judgment of the universal body
of bishops which God established as the infallible means for ascertaining that truth (*Works*, II, 81). Thus, for England voluntaryism was
not only an individual's freedom of belief -- a rule of persuasion rather
than coercion in matters of faith -- and the right and responsibility to
support the church, but also the liberty to form voluntary associations
and the right to a specifically limited amount of participation and
power within those institutions.

CHAPTER IV

political *republicanism*

Just as England maintained that religious liberty, separation, and voluntaryism were consistent with Catholic principles and practices, so also he asserted that the general political ideology of republicanism was compatible with Catholic thinking. He declared that Catholics were free to hold their own individual views on the nature of political government. Because it was not a subject of revelation, the church had no official position. The source of all government was part of the natural human law and not the divine law. Therefore, men were free to decide which form of government best suited their own circumstances. Although he supported every Catholic's right to his own opinion on the nature of political governments, England declared that some Catholics were in the forefront in advocating republicanism in the past, both as a political theory and even as a form of ecclesiastical government. When England wanted to show that the Catholic Church was not opposed to republican political principles, he quoted from Thomas Aquinas, Robert Bellarmine, Francisco de Suarez, a number of other catholic theologians, and some church councils. Many Catholic writers, he stated, had held the opinion that the people were the only legitimate source of all civil authority and government. The 1431 Council of Basel, for example, used this theory of government in trying to solve the problem of the relationship of the pope to the entire church. The Basel Council Fathers held that,

> The pope is in his church as a king in his kingdom;
> and for a king to be of more authority than his
> kingdom, it were too absurd, -- ergo [sic] neither
> ought the Pope to be above his church (*Works*, IV, 95).

Even though he used numerous Catholic sources, England preferred Bellarmine to others on the nature of government and frequently quoted his *De Romano Pontifice*. England believed that Bellarmine's theory of government most closely approximated American republicanism. Bellarmine, for example, favored a mixed form of government which accepted the best of each traditional type. He believed that an institution which contained elements of a monarchy, an aristocracy and a democracy was "the best and most desirable form of government." In describing the role of the executive in a mixed government, England quoted Bellarmine:

> There should be some President who should have authority
> over all, and be subject to no person: also governors of
> Provinces or States, let them not be Vicars of any king,
> nor annual judges, but true Presidents, who shall at the
> same time be obedient to the authority of the chief
> President, and each govern his own Province or State, not
> as that of a stranger, but as his own.... But if we add
> to this, that neither this principal nor these lesser
> Presidents, should acquire their dignities by any *hereditary
> succession*; but that the best persons should be raised
> thereto, by the choice of the whole people; there would
> then in this commonwealth, be given its proper weight
> to the principle of Democracy.[14]

England believed this description of the executive was not very different from the office of the President of the United States. He, of course, read Bellarmine's analysis of the *Princeps* within the context of the American experience and did not attempt to give an historical exegesis of Bellarmine's theory of government. England was using him only to sustain his own view that Catholic writers had given ideological support to republican governments.

CHAPTER II

the provincial councils

England's prominence in establishing what has become known as the American conciliar tradition has long been recognized.[11] What has not been so clearly understood is that England's fathering of the conciliar practices was based upon his moderate conciliarism, and his republican constitutional views of the church. While attempting to convince Archbishop Marechal of the need to call provincial councils in the United States, he clearly revealed much of his republican constitutional-mentality.

According to England, a provincial council was not simply an instrument for the practical government of the church; it was an effective visible means for manifesting the unity and catholicity of the Catholic Church. Although the national church was one in spirit, doctrine, and worship, it had no way of demonstrating its internal solidarity and universality without provincial councils. In a way, the councils sacramentally revealed and effected not only a stronger harmony but also a more potent collaboration on the common problems of the national Catholic community.

England felt that the Catholic Church in the United States, before the convocation of the first Provincial Council of Baltimore in 1829, was "the worst organized church in our states." A provincial council provided for a nationally-organized system within the church, the essential points of which were "community of counsel and unity of action" (*Works*, II, 374). In an 1827 letter to Archbishop Marechal, England asked the prelate to consider the advantages of such provincial councils for the American Catholic Church.

> Whether the spirit of the Church does not recommend
> and the canons require synods. Whether it is not very
> necessary that we should know each other, confide in
> each other and be united to each other whilst our
> adversaries are combined systematically against us.
> Whether we have any national discipline. Whether it is
> not fit to make a commencement. Whether we are not
> already becoming a separated number of Pastors
> without any spirit of unity, unity of custom, unity of
> discipline, unity of action, unity of purpose, unity of
> affection. Whether in any one sense of the word we
> form a national Church save in name (AAB, April 26,
> 1827; cf. Guilday 1927: II, 104).

In England's mind a provincial council was a means of reducing the principles of unity and catholicity to practice.[12] The problems as well as the resources of one diocese belonged to the whole church. Each church was united to every other church by common bonds of faith and love. That the American church become organized through provincial synods where common concerns and resources could be mutually shared, therefore, was imperative.

> The special evils of each [diocese], are in some measure
> a common concern for the whole and that this has been
> acknowledged by the Church from the beginning, as an
> undoubted principle felt through all its Provinces
> (England to Marechal, June 25, 1827 in AAB; Guilday
> 1927: II, 108).

England's call for provincial councils was based upon "catholic principles of ancient discipline" (England to Rosati, Rothensteiner 1927: 270). Early Christian conciliar practices acknowledged and carried out the true spiritual mission in the church. The authority exercised in these councils,

> is not that of moral persuasion alone, but a spiritual
> power communicated by the Saviour to his Apostles
> and their successors, for preserving truth in doctrine,

order and subordination in the external government of the Church (*USCM*, Nov. 2, 1833: 142).

The ancient councils manifested the true purpose of the church in preserving unity in truth, order, charity among the different churches, and cooperation in meeting the universal needs and sufferings of the different churches.

The value of the ancient practices was also acknowledged in the decrees of the Council of Trent (Sess. 24, *de. Ref.* chp. 2, in *USCM*, IX, pp. 174, 242, 295). This council's recommendation of triennial provincial councils was enough legal precedent for England to call upon the archbishop to convoke regular synods. Since the Council of Trent, England maintained, few provincial councils were held in the various countries of Europe:

In most of the countries of Europe, the tyranny exercised over the church, under the pretext of its protection, has extended so far as to prevent such assemblies and, therefore, during centuries, comparatively few provincial councils have been held in Spain, Portugal, France or Germany (*USCM*, May 13, 1837: 350).

Although churches in other countries, persecuted by temporal governments, may have had sufficient reasons for not holding regular councils since Trent, the church in the United States had no valid excuse for not complying with the Tridentine decree.

In Ireland, however, where the church had been persecuted for centuries, the bishops found it necessary to meet periodically -- in the bogs and glens when no other place was available or safe.[13] At the present time, England asserted, the frequent, yearly meetings of the national Irish Episcopacy had created order and promoted the progress of religion in Ireland (England to Rosati, Sept. 18, 1832, in Rothensteiner 1927: 267; cf. also *USCM*, Jan. 25, 1834: 238). In the United States, the freedom provided by the American Constitution should have encouraged the re-establishment of the regular practice of holding provincial councils.

Alluding to Archbishop Carroll, England called for the "revival or rather the completion and the execution" of provincial councils. According to England, Carroll "who better than most others knew and loved the American Church" saw the particular usefulness and necessity of provincial councils for promoting a nationally-organized church (*USCM*, Dec. 27, 1828: 199; cf. also *USCM*, May 3, 1828: 342).

The provincial council, for England, would symbolize the unity, ecclesiastical independence, and maturity of a national American
Catholic Church. The American church, he told Marechal, should not
be governed in local matters by the Roman Church, but rather, like
every mature church, should regulate its own discipline. Although he
acknowledged his respect for Rome as "the mother and mistress of all
churches," he still thought that it was

> in the nature of things impossible for the tribunals in
> Rome to know, as well as the Bishops of America, the
> discipline most beneficial to the American Church
> (England to Marechal, June 25, 1827, in AAB; cf. also
> Guilday 1927: II, 109).

Provincial councils should also be established because they
manifested to the American people the "republican part of church
government" (Ibid.). A provincial council demonstrated system, order
and subordination within the church. England realized that Americans
valued law and system, not arbitrary power nor episcopal mandates.
He felt that "each [American] bishop had practically greater power in
his own diocese than the Pope had in the Universal Church." Bishops in
the United States had all the powers they were capable of possessing
"without any Congregation, or Council or established discipline, to
limit their exercise" (Papers Relating 1897: 460). "In plain practice, "
England wrote to a friend, "at present [1828] every American Diocese
is a Popedom" (England to Simon Brute, June 4, 1828, in Guilday
1927: II, 110, n. 44). England believed provincial councils could
restrain this excessive episcopal authority. He therefore sought to have
the American church governed upon what William Read called "the
true Catholic principle of governing by episcopal legislation, instead of
that of episcopal dictation" (Works, I, 17). In England's mind this
practice was "in accordance with the spirit of our National
institutions" (England to Marechal, June 25, 1827; in Guilday 1927: II,
109). He felt that the provincial system of church government con-
formed to the principles of American government and that their
similarity was so striking that "it would easily gain not only their [the
American Catholics'] obedience but also their attachment" (Papers
Relating 1897: 462). The provincial form of church government,
moreover, like American republicanism, provided for common consultation and deliberation before legislation. England valued "as well
from feeling as from principle" common deliberations that led to concrete decisions. In another context, he described the benefits of common consultation:

...since I prefer the collected experience and reasoning
of the bulk of society to the results of my own weak efforts, I believe it to be the suggestion of reason, and
the duty of an individual, to admit that he is not as
wise as is the collective body of his fellow men. I am,
therefore, prepared to view most favorably, and with
what I call a fair partiality, any practice with [sic] the
great body of reasonable and honorable men after
natural reflection, and as the expression of their judgment, and not of their prejudices, will say is necessary,
or even useful to preserve the order of society, and the
decorum of civil intercourse (Works, V, 65; cf. also
USCM, June 9, 1832: 398).

After the provincial councils were finally established, some
American bishops feared that England wanted to introduce
republicanism into the government of the national church and thereby
weaken their episcopal authority.[14] After the first council, England
tried to calm those fears by indicating the compatibility between
republicanism and Catholic Church government. He pointed out that
blind obedience did not exist even in the church. He stated that the
bishops had nothing to fear from the independence of republican-
minded men. For him obedience and independence were not at
odds, since subordination was a part of the just constitutional demands
of every republic. Republicans were not independent of all law and
authority: they rejected only arbitrary power; they respected and were
obedient to written laws and constitutional definitions of duties.
England saw that the provincial councils were a blending of republican
freedoms and religious obedience.

Fortunately for our prelates they have not to frame a
new form of government, but only to put in execution
as far as practicable, regulations sanctioned by the experience of ages. He is the best champion of well-
regulated liberty who most strenuously upholds the
force and vigour of the law, and he best secures
freedom who supports regularly established authority
(USCM, March 13, 1830: 294).

According to England, provincial councils recommended themselves
not only to the liberal considerations of American republicans, but also
to American Protestants. The councils were similar to the forms of
government used by the American Protestants who had adopted the

"catholic principle of ancient discipline" in "their monthly, yearly and triennial meetings of presbyteries, synods, assemblies, conferences, conventions, and societies" (England to Rosati, Rothensteiner 1927: 270; cf. also *Works*, V, 422). Through these practices, Protestantism made great progress. If Catholics were to unify they could achieve similar success.

England believed, moreover, that the provincial synod could be an effective means in relating the true nature of Catholicism to the Protestant public. Before the first provincial meeting in 1829, he tried to anticipate the good effects of the synod in this regard.

> The more our principles are developed and made
> known, the greater publicity is given to the evidences
> upon which our faith is based, and our hopes for eter-
> nal happiness are grounded the more do our brethren,
> who differ with us in the faith, acknowledge the force
> of the one and duly appreciate and admire the other...
> What cheers us most of all in our flattering anticipa-
> tions of the future advances of the Catholic religion in
> this country, is the idea of happy effects likely to result
> from the Synod of our Bishops, to be held the present
> month in Baltimore (*USCM*, Oct. 3, 1829: 110).

The first provincial council did not fulfill England's fond expectations. On the contrary, it increased Protestant fears of Catholicism.[15]

Although England's insistence and persistence helped to establish and maintain a regular conciliar government of the American Catholic Church,[16] nevertheless his personal success within the councils was, ironically, extremely limited. Most of his specific conciliar proposals for the church in the United States failed to receive majority support among the bishops. By his own admission, corroborated by Bishop Francis Kenrick, England always voted with the minority on specific controversial issues in the American church.[17] He had hoped the provincial councils would establish legislation which would acknowledge the rights and duties of all in the church -- bishops, priests and people. The opposite, in fact, occurred. Episcopal rights and duties were confirmed while clerical and lay rights were severely restricted or almost completely ignored.[18] He wanted the laity in particular to become a more integral part of the episcopal deliberations and national legislation,[19] but that happened only during the first council when lay legal experts were brought in to advise the bishops on American laws regarding church property. The American bishops rejected England's constitutional efforts. Some, in fact, felt that he was trying to force his own diocesan constitutional procedures upon national ecclesiastical government. England protested that he only wanted to explain how it worked in his diocese and what it had accomplished (England to Eccleston, Feb. 7, 1840, in AAB). But the objection did not calm the bishops' fears of his radical and "innovative" procedures in church government.[20] England tried to establish conciliar voting procedures which would follow the example "of all other judicial bodies." He suggested the voting start with the junior member of the hierarchy and then proceed to the senior members. This proposal, the bishops also rejected (*USCM*, May 23, 1840: 266-67). Most of the attempts he made to bring the synodal procedures more in line with republican and American constitutional practices likewise failed. In 1834, after the second provincial council, he wrote to Paul Cullen in Rome informing him that he and the other American bishops had opposite ideas and ideals on the nature of the church government.

> They [the American bishops] are well disposed but
> their minds and mine are cast in different moulds, and
> cooperation is out of the question; for I cannot approve
> of their principles of administration, and at the last
> Council, they plainly manifested the most distinct want
> of confidence in me (May 13, 1834, in Papers Relating
> 1896: 481; cf. also Guilday 1927: I, 537).

Although England failed at the provincial and national levels to bring ecclesiastical government into conformity with his ideas of constitutionality and his ideals of republican government, he generally succeeded in his own diocese in accomplishing these same goals.

CHAPTER III

the diocesan church

John England's republican-constitutional view of the church becomes most evident in the government of his own diocese. There he felt he had the freedom to adapt the government to the needs and temperament of his people while maintaining essential unity with the general government and discipline of the universal church. The preceding section revealed the republican elements of his constitutional form of government; the following paragraphs show the conciliar or collegial dimension of his republicanism.

England made his collegial concept of the church visible in the annual conventions which provided a method for effectively expressing and experiencing the communal nature of the church. The constitution of the diocese taught Catholic principles of unity and diversity, but the annual conventions effected what the constitution taught. For England, the conventions were the primary vehicle in his diocese for revealing the church as the body of Christ. In his 1827 address to the Georgia Convention, he outlined the Catholic principles upon which the constitution-convention system of church government was based:

> It was always a maxim in the church to preserve her
> children in charity and affection, as brethren dwelling

together in unity...she draws her children together as
one family, having in view one great object, and striv-
ing together to establish peace, harmony, and affection
on earth, as they seek to attain the enjoyment of one
glory in the kingdom of their father in a better world.
The Saviour declared to them, by this shall men know
that you are my disciples, if you love one another. To
bring together in affection and charity, the clergy and
the principal laity of the state at specified periods, so as
to make them feel that they were one body, so as to afford them an opportunity of kind intercourse, and bind
them together by a more firm league of confidence was
thought to be highly useful; their union for a common
purpose creates confidence, enkindles zeal, and
animates to exertion (*Works*, IV, 386).

According to England, the constitutional form of government not only
solved the problems generated by the trustee crisis, but it also fulfilled
the purposes for which the church was created:

...it has prevented discord, it has banished jealousy, it
has secured peace, it has produced efforts of cooperation, and established mutual confidence and affection
between our several churches, as well as between the
pastors and their flocks, and between the bishop and
the churches (*Works*, IV, 357).

During his day, and even recently, England was accused of following Protestant principles and practices in establishing his constitutional
form of church government.[21] England's bi-cameral system of church
government was certainly similar to that of the South Carolina Protestant Episcopal Church in the United States at the time. For England,
however, that similarity did not mean that his system was based on
Protestant principles. Rather, he believed that the Protestant practices
of church government in the United States, especially their yearly conventions and national meetings, were based, on the contrary, upon
Catholic or primitive Christian principles.[22] By appropriating the
republican and Protestant practices of government, England believed
that he was imitating the ancient conciliar principles and practices.
Even though the annual conventions were not strictly conciliar in
the canonical sense of the word, their organization and procedures
were at least analogous to the legislative methods found in republican

governments, ecclesiastical chapters, and church councils. The delegates to the convention were elected by majority vote; they, like members of the cathedral chapters, were considered "a body of sage, prudent, and religious counsellors" to aid the bishop in the administration of the diocese; and, as in conciliar gatherings, the annual conventions were not simply a means for the communal government of the diocese; they were ecclesial and liturgical events.[23] Everything during the convocations was done in the context of worship. The annual meetings always opened with a celebration of Mass, at which time each of the elected representatives of the diocese made a solemn public promise before the gathered assembly that he would observe and maintain the doctrine and discipline of the Catholic Church, abide by the provisions of the constitution, and carry out the decisions of the convention (USCM, VI, 198; Diurnal, 210). The liturgical context made the promise to serve in the government of the church a religious commitment, not simply a perfunctory administrative obligation. The liturgical nature of the conventions also made manifest the relationship between worship and ecclesiastical government. The business meetings which followed the opening celebration of the liturgy related the act of worship to the communal responsibility for the church's government and mission. In such a juxtaposition, church government and mission could be seen as the continuation and extension of worship. Major diocesan liturgical events, moreover, were celebrated each year during the time of the conventions when the whole church was most visibly manifested. The bishop held ordinations to the minor orders and to the priesthood during the assemblies. Periodically, he would celebrate a special mass for the dead during this time, either for members of the diocese who had died during the previous year or for a deceased pope or some other church dignitary. Furthermore, at the conclusion of every yearly gathering, which lasted between three and four days, the delegates would again meet with the bishop in a liturgical ceremony where he would confirm their acts, resolutions and administrative decisions. Thus, the annual convention was conducted as an ecclesial and liturgical event.

The conventions made the delegates more aware of the universal as well as the local church. The yearly meetings themselves demonstrated to the representatives that the church was more than the local congregation. The assembly was first of all an opportunity for the isolated Catholics of the diocese to make themselves known to each other and to the bishop (Works, IV, 384). It also enabled them to confess their faith in public, a great difficulty prior to the gatherings because of the fear engendered by their minority status in the South.[24] The convention

helped to remove the fear and provided a basis for a more comprehensive view of the entire church (*USCM*, Nov. 24, 1824: 329). In his yearly addresses, England tried to enlarge the delegates' vision by making
them aware of the broader needs of the entire diocese and of the
universal church. He repeatedly reminded them of exigencies beyond
the individual parishes (e.g., the diocesan seminary, supply of priests,
mission work, schools for all members of the various communities,
etc.). These services were vital to the interest of the local communities
but could be supplied only by a united effort. In his own words, the
convention provided a means for collecting together "the knowledge of
facts, the advantage of the experience, and the opinions of the
members of the several churches, to provide for their common interests
by the united zeal and information of the whole" (*Works*, IV, 386).

England frequently spoke of the connection between the "churches"
and the "church." These terms referred at times to the harmony between the local congregations and the diocese, at other times to the relationship between the diocesan church and the universal Roman Communion. Through the annual conventions and through the use of these
Pauline terms for the church, he intended to keep the local churches and
the universal church in communion and in a healthy tension.

THE BISHOP

England shared many of his colleagues' perceptions on a monarchical episcopacy. He viewed the bishop at the father who embodied
all the legislative, judicial, and executive powers in the diocese and as
such officially interpreted the gospel for the local church.

England also perceived the theological distinction between the laity
and all clergy in traditional terms. The God-given difference between
the laity and the clergy, "a distinction which even the Calvinists
uphold" (*Works*, II, 493), arose from the fact that some were officially
commissioned and sent to preach the gospel publicly while others were
not (*Works*, II, 478). The Waldensians, for example, had "usurped"
the ministry of preaching by evangelizing without the proper commission or qualifications. The dissimilarity between the laity and the
clergy resulted from the proper Apostolic commission which created a
"dignity" in the priesthood (according to Augustine, Jerome,
Chrysostom and other holy fathers of the church) "superior to that not
only of kings themselves but even of angels and archangels"(*Works*, I,
252). Priestly "exaltation," however, "was for example, not for
domination."[25] The divine commission to bishops and priests gave them

"precedence of ecclesiastical authority" but not "precedence in society, nor in virtue" (*Works*, V, 164). The bishop's authority in the church, therefore, could not be completely compared to that in a republican state:

> The authority to preside and to teach in the church of
> God is not derived from talents, nor from wealth, nor
> from worldly power, nor from popular choice, nor
> even from the piety and virtue of the individual, but
> from his having been regularly assumed to the
> apostleship, and ordained therefore by some successor
> of an apostle who has thereby received his authority
> from Jesus Christ (*Works*, IV, 233).

England taught the accepted Catholic doctrine on religious subordination and submission; but he always emphasized that all within the church -- clergy and laity alike -- were equally subject to Christ's power, the sacraments, the universal church's interpretation of scriptures, and to the church's teachings, written laws, and discipline. Here, no distinction existed between pope, priest or Catholic pauper. In the republican society in which they lived, England believed that the American Catholics knew how to preserve "unity of faith, religious subordination, political freedom of opinion and action, and republican independence with becoming respect for those with whom they differ" (*Works*, IV, 90; I, 184). In that free society, however, all religious subordination should be reasonable. Bishops and other clerics should above all be men of competence and personal merit; their expertise should win for them the free submission and support of their laity, and their commands should be given and sustained with reasons (Papers Relating, 1897: 461).

Although England shared many of the traditional ideas on a monarchical episcopacy, nevertheless he differed significantly from his episcopal colleagues in his perception as well as his exercise of the episcopal role. His constitutionalism, in particular, modified considerably the traditional monarchical view and attempted to change the episcopal image in American society. For him, the bishop was a constitutionally-limited governor who presided over and operated within a precisely defined constitutional religious community, facilitated unity and cooperation, and supervised the formation of the Catholic Church in the South. At times he functioned only with the consent of the community, but always with its advice and cooperation. Thus, through the processes of shared responsibility for the upbuilding of the church, he developed a new image of a constitutional, rather than a purely monarchical, episcopate

In view of England's concept of the bishop, his emphasis upon
Catholic republicanism, and his previous advocacy of domestic
nomination in Ireland, it would seem logical that he would have promoted some kind of clerical nomination of bishops to vacant sees in the
United States. Such, however, was not the case. He was not altogether
against some form of clerical nomination, but he did not demand it in
the United States as he had as a priest in Ireland. In fact, contrary to
his former position, he maintained, much the same as Maréchal had in
his 1819 *Pastoral* to the Norfolk Trustees, that the "right" to elect the
bishop never existed in the church, even though permission for such
elections had been granted.[26] In the church's present practice, England
asserted against the trustees, permission and privilege had been
withheld. It had been withdrawn, he believed, because such elections
in the past had caused dissension, contention, animosity, tumult and a
breach of the peace (*Works*, V, 153; cf. Kenrick 1843: 21-22). Anyone
who viewed the existing troubles of the church in Philadelphia, he
declared, would see the reasonableness of withholding such suffrages
from the priests and people. When the Philadelphia trustees and priests
referred to the election of Bishop Carroll by his priests, England
responded that the pope had granted the priests the power of such election for one time only -- he had no intention of establishing a precedent. At any rate the laity were in no way included in the first election
of a bishop in the United States.[27]

Although most of England's public replies to the question of the election of bishops by priests and people were negative, some of his private
letters reveal that he still favored a form of clerical participation.[28] At
the time of his death in 1842, he requested that the priests of his diocese
should each write to the archbishop and other bishops of the province
to indicate whom they desired to replace him (*Works*, I, 19). Other
than these brief references to clerical participation in domestic
nominations, England remained strangely silent in contrast to his
public advocacy for these rights in Ireland. The trustee controversy
was no doubt primarily responsible for his reticence in this area.

THE PRIEST

Although England was not a forceful public advocate for domestic
nominations, he was an articulate supporter of other clerical rights.[29]
He seems to have perceived the role of the American priest much in the
same way he viewed that of the bishop in the church. Like the bishop,
the priest was a divinely-commissioned instrument of salvation in the
local community.

> His [the priest's] situation is not like that of a profes-
> sional man, to whom you may have recourse, if you
> will, or from amongst several of whom you can select
> him whom you would prefer. No: -- the clergyman is
> your pastor, commissioned to teach you the doctrines of
> religion, to guide you in the way of virtue, to offer up
> the holy sacrifice on your behalf, and to administer to
> you the sacraments which the Saviour has instituted
> (*Works*,IV, 438-39).

England's traditional theological view of the function of the priest, like that of his perception of the episcopal role, was modfed by his ideas on priestly ministry within a constitutionally organized American Catholic congregation.

What the bishop was to the diocesan church, the priest was to the local congregation. The priest was a presiding officer of the local parish; he had his religious counsellors, the vestry members who were elected representatives of the parish, from whom he received advice and with whom he shared responsibility for the functioning of the parish unit. His position in the local parish, however, differed from that of the bishop in the diocese, in that he did not have absolute veto power over the decisions and votes of the vestry. In certain cases of financial administration the vote of the majority of the vestrymen was sufficient to override the vote of the priest (*Works*, V, 103).

In the administration of general diocesan affairs, the priest was seen as a cooperator with the bishop and the laity. In virtue of his office as priest he was a religious counsellor to the bishop. During the yearly conventions he had the right and the duty to offer his opinions publicly on the state of the diocese and to vote on issues where he had constitutional competence.

The priest was also seen as an agent of provincial decisions. After each provincial council, the diocesan priests met in diocesan synods to discuss the provincial statutes and to determine how they should be applied to the diocese. Some provincial decrees were regulatory and therefore were simply made a part of diocesan legislation; others, however, were only admonitory and recommendatory. The priests discussed the practicality and feasibility of the latter laws and modified them to fit diocesan circumstances. After discussing provincial legislation, the priests helped the bishop create legislation pertaining specifically to clerical affairs. During the first Charleston diocesan synod, for example, the priests presented a proposal to create a fund for the support of "the infirm, decayed or destitute priests of the diocese." After debating the issue, the members of the synod agreed to provide a

regular procedure for the financial assistance of retired clergy. A fund
was established from the voluntary donations of the active clergy
which would be increased and sustained by yearly assessments upon
priests (*USCM*, Nov. 27, 1831: 174). On regulations such as this the
synods provided for clerical participation in legislation that related to
their own lives.

In the Charleston diocese, furthermore, England invited the assistant pastors as well as the rectors to participate in the synods. He did not
acknowledge, however, that the assistants had a right to attend the
synods; they were participants only by way of episcopal favor.
Through the diocesan synods and other attempts to incorporate the
clergy into the total mission of the diocese, England seems to have gained the whole-hearted cooperation of his priests.[30]

Priests, according to England, were partners with the bishop and the
laity in the religious life and government of the local congregation and
the diocesan church. They were also, however, citizens of a free state.
As such, they had temporal and political responsibilities. They were to
be exemplary citizens; in the United States, however, unlike in Ireland,
they were not to interfere in politics since the state did not oppress
religion. Varying social and political circumstances, England believed,
demanded different clerical roles and responsibilities. The priests'
functions in society were not absolutely predetermined; they were conditioned by the times. In the United States, the clergy were simply to
call the laity to obey the Christian virtues, to instill sentiments of love
and patriotism, and to exemplify the virtues of committed free citizens
(*Works*, V, 143-45).

THE LAITY

England's theological conception of the role of the laity in the
church, like his perception of the ministry of the bishop and priest, was
simultaneously traditional and innovative. His constitution and his
apologetical writings emphasized repeatedly that as individuals and as
members of the church, laity and clergy had the same Christian dignity
and the same Christian rights; however, they did not have the same
sacramental commission and jurisdictional functions. In the constitution England asserted that the laity had no power or authority in the
government of the church.

> We do not believe that our Lord Jesus Christ gave to
> the faithful at large the government of the church nor

any power to regulate spiritual or ecclesiastical concerns; neither do we believe that he gave to the laity
nor to any part of the laity such government nor such
power nor any portion of such government or such
power (*Works*, V, 95).

Although England denied the laity's governing powers or rights in the
church, nevertheless his constitution and convention system contained
a new awareness of the Catholic layman's role in a republican environment. The collegial-republican nature of the constitution was in itself a
recognition of the new role of the laity in the church. Even though the
Catholic layman had no explicit jurisdictional powers in the government of the church, except in temporal matters, his advice and counsel
were necessary, England felt, for the smooth and effective administration of the local church. In England's eyes the Catholic layman was a
participating partner in the temporal and spiritual work of the church.
The laymen had freedoms and rights within the church, were independent of the clergy in political matters, and had special experiences and
expertise of the world to offer in the upbuilding of the church (*Works*,
IV, 386). All in all, the layman was a republican Christian in that he
could exercise his role by publicly participating in the total mission of
the local church.[31]

England won the support of his laity through the constitution and his
other exertions for Catholic religion in the South. Almost yearly the lay
delegates to the conventions expressed their gratitude for England's
ministry in their diocese. In 1832, they sent him the following letter of
appreciation:

There is a more solemn voice which comes from the
embodied spirit of thousands; it is the voice of your
church -- of your people. For them you have accomplished that for which they must be ever thankful.
Right Rev. Sir, when you first came amongst us, we
were poor and weak; we were indeed as sheep without
a shepherd; congregated within a small space, suffering
without resistance, the encroachments of our every foe;
and looking almost without hope to the time when we
would be gathered to our fathers, and be thus pro-
tected from the religious prejudices of those who
taunted us, and even followed us with sneers to the
very foot of the consecrated altar. But, that providence
which declared "I will be with thee to the end," sent
one to succour us at a time, when we were faint and

dying; when we were distracted in our councils and
neglectful of our holy duties. Actuated by a devoted
love to the service of Christ, you then came to us; you
identified your fortunes with ours; you shared our
labours, you suffered our wants, and by your fortitude
and energy taught us how to bear them. From this
time our affairs began to brighten. Abuses were corrected; our expenditures were regulated by the strictest
economy; the organization of the church in your
diocese was commenced and has been completed; the
duties of your flock were pointed out, explained and
observed; and instead of being tossed as for many years
we had been, upon a sea of uncertainty, the beacon
you raised soon guided us to that rock whereon the
great God hath built his universal church (*USCM*, July
7, 1832; 6).

In spirit and ideology, the laity and England were united. They were
particularly in accord on seeing the relationship between the Catholic
Church and republican institutions. The lay delegates, like England,
periodically sent circular letters to the people of the diocese to show
how even in administrative procedures and resources "the spirit of our
church is...in accordance with the spirit of republic institutions."[32]

What separated England, however, from some of the laity of his
diocese and from almost all the trustees in the United States was the
issue of lay patronage. England denied that the laity had any right to
nominate their own pastors. He acknowledged that they should have a
voice in rejecting pastors whom they could not tolerate; but he felt that
trustee claims for the rights of patronage were the primary cause of all
the unfortunate schisms in the church in the United States (*USCM*,
Dec. 18, 1822: 231). He also believed that "the canons which gave the
right of lay-patronage are very bad."[33]

England's constitution, as indeed his entire approach to accommodating the Catholic Church to American conditions, was based
upon a republican-constitutional view of the church. That perception
was a blending of republican political principles and Catholic constitutionalism. Even though England stressed the external elements of order
and government in his descriptions of the church, nevertheless he
grounded that emphasis on the Pauline image of the church as the body
of Christ. He acknowledged in particular the unity and legitimate
diversity within the universal church, and the proper distinction of
functions and rights within the national and diocesan church. Like
some of the moderate conciliarists of the Council of Constance, he ap-

plied constitutional restraints to the relationship between the pope and a general council; unlike many of them, however, he extended this application to the entire church, especially to the national and local church. (The American republican environment was in part responsible for this latter tendency.) He combined his republicanism and Catholic constitutionalism to create a new image of the Catholic Church and a new pastoral role for the bishop, clergy and laity in the American church.

England perceived the church as a constitutional community of believing persons in which the rights and responsibilities of all were properly defined and thereby restrained. Within this body of believers, even though all shared the same Christian dignity and were equally witnesses to the Christian tradition, certain members had special roles. Because England saw the local bishop as a constitutionally-limited governor, he presented the bishop more as a presiding officer than as the only governing official in the diocesan church. The bishop was the facilitator of unity and peace, the defender of Catholicism, the court of appeal in local disputes, the friend and associate of the priests and laymen, the partner with them in determining the management and use of the church's temporalities and in building up the church in the country, and the final judge of the Christian tradition in the local church. The priest was the bishop's representative in the local parish, an advisor in diocesan affairs, a legislative assistant in regard to administering provincial and diocesan laws, and a consort with the laity and the bishop in congregational and diocesan ecclesiastical concerns. The layman, like the priest, was an active witness to the Christian tradition in the United States, a religious counsellor in congregational and diocesan matters relating to the general welfare of the church, and a responsible collaborator with the bishop and the clergy in the life and administration of the parish and diocese.

England's concept of the church responded to the primary question of the day: the relationship of Catholicism to the new experience of republicanism. The American environment forced him to re-examine his understanding of the church. In the process, he emphasized those elements in the church's tradition which corresponded most closely to the American milieu: democracy, representation, lay participation, constitutionality, subordination and freedom. His Irish political and ecclesiastical experiences had prepared him more than any other bishop in the American church to look favorably upon these characteristics of Catholic theology and practice. In his own mind, he succeeded in reconciling the conceptual and practical relationship between American republicanism and Catholicism. He failed to convince many American Protestants, however, that the two were compatible because, among other things, he presented his own conception of the church as if it were the Catholic view, whereas, in reality, it was found in practice only in his own diocese. It was neither the perception nor the practice of the majority of the episcopacy at the time. England, moreover, did not succeed in harmonizing republicanism and Catholicism in the formation of the national church. His efforts to establish the provincial councils had the ironical effect of implanting an episcopal aristocracy rather than bringing the national church into conformity with American institutions. Thus, because most bishops at the time rejected the attempt to reconcile Catholicism with republicanism, England's constitutionalism, although generally successful in his own diocese, did not endure there after his death nor did it influence the direction of the national church.

SECTION V

conclusions

From John England's arrival in 1820 until his death in 1842, American Catholicism was gradually but steadily transformed from a low profile, numerically insignificant, and nationally-unorganized minority into an increasingly numerous, aggressively self-defensive, and well-organized national community. Bishop John England and Immigrant Irish Catholicism played a major role in the dramatic change. During these years of serious internal dissent and severe external harrassment, England -- as an immigrant bishop, theologian, and political commentator -- became one of the primary articulators of an Irish-American Catholic identity, the chief spokesman for a liberal Irish-Catholic tradition, and the foremost builder of a constitutional American Catholicism. Although he never convinced the nativists that Catholicism and American republicanism were compatible, he equipped the incipient immigrant Catholic community with a sense of identity as Americans and as Catholics. He also provided Catholics with a religious meaning system which helped them to relate to the new world of republicanism and supported them during the trials of nativism and the chaos caused by trusteeism. As a first generation Irish immigrant, moreover, he laid the foundations for the Irish Catholic's easy assimilation into American society, even though this was itself a cause of tension with immigrants of other national backgrounds.

In five ways England and Irish Catholicism contributed to the formation of an American Catholic consciousness and the development of institutional structures. First, England and other Irish immigrants formulated an American Catholic ideology on religious liberty -- a position consistent with the liberal principles they had inherited from their Irish political and religious experiences. Unfortunately for the American Catholic community's relationship with the American Protestant majority, these ideas were considered unorthodox in much of the Catholic world at the time. Thus, nativist Protestants justifiably charged that American Catholic professions of religious liberty were contradicted by papal teachings. Catholics failed to answer these charges adequately and, thereby, intensified hostilities between themselves and the nativists throughout much of the nineteenth and twentieth centuries. Despite protestations to the contrary, the first generation Irish immigrants did believe that religious liberty was as Catholic as it was American. Such a belief was a significant part of their minority identity -- a part of their self definition which the nativist majority could not accept.

In the United States, issues like religious liberty and voluntaryism referred not only to the relationship between the church and state but also to the freedom of the Christian within voluntary ecclesiastical organizations. As much as England tried through his diocesan constitution and apologetical writings, he was unable to persuade American nativists that true freedom existed within the Catholic Church. Many of his episcopal colleagues were likewise not swayed by his professions of ecclesiastical freedom and considered them rash accommodations to the liberty-loving spirit of the times. The hostilities of trusteeism and the rigorous episcopal legislation against clerical and lay participation militated against England's attempts in this area. His apologetics had substance only in his own diocese; outside his constitutional government, however, freedom and participation within the Catholic community were severely restricted. After England's day, others would take up the call for internal freedom and participation -- with a corresponding lack of success.

Second, England's advocacy of the separation of church and state not only articulated the position of his fellow Irish immigrants but also formulated the principles held by a majority in the American Catholic community. His own particular interpretation of the consequences of a radical separation, moreover, had three profound and lasting effects upon the formation of the American Catholic Church. First of all, his interpretation, which was accepted by most of his contemporary episcopal colleagues, contributed to the failure of episcopal moral leadership in American society.[1] For him, the church was responsible for man's spiritual welfare and for inculcating the moral virtues of citizenship and patriotism; the state took care of man's civil welfare. In practice the church was the handmaid of American civil religion; Catholics, therefore, became enthusiastic and uncritical supporters of American political institutions and decisions. The bishops, moreover, exercised no moral leadership upon political matters. They refused to take a stand on slavery and the wars against the Indians, for example, because for them these issues were political (see Carey 1975: 231).

England's interpretation of separation also contributed to the development of separate Catholic social welfare institutions. Although the church had no direct competence in political affairs, it did have a responsibility for the Catholic's social and temporal welfare. The ideological basis of this stance can be found in England's conception of a Catholic society distinct from American society. Because the church subsisted as a separate and perfect society within the larger American community, it had to establish its own social programs. This did not mean, as already mentioned, that Catholicism was a critical force upon American society, only that it was a separate entity within that community. The perception of the church as an autonomous community contributed to the establishment of separate Catholic schools and other institutions for the care of American Catholics' social and temporal needs.

Ironically, England's interpretation of the two separate societies in America provided a justification for the American Catholic bishops' refusal to accommodate Catholicism to republican principles, except in the area of episcopal conciliar practices. His interpretation sustained the position that the Catholic Church could subsist in American republicanism without appropriating the principles and practices of that society. Thus, England's view of separation supported his opponents' opposition to American Catholic constitutionalism and assisted them in forming the American church along rigidly monarchic and aristocratic rather than republican lines.

Besides religious liberty and separation, the Irish principle and practice of voluntaryism contributed greatly not only to the Irish Catholics' easy assimilation into American religious experiences, but also to the development of nineteenth-century American Catholicism. The establishment of private educational systems, social welfare agencies and hospitals, as well as the evolution of the brick and mortar mentality in American Catholicism resulted primarily from Irish voluntaryism. The first-generation Irish experience, moreover, served as an example for later immigrant Catholic communities. England, like many of his episcopal and clerical successors, frequently appealed to this tradition. Unlike some of his successors, however, he emphasized that the practice of voluntaryism was grounded in spiritual soil. Religion for him was based upon spiritual persuasion; the physical development of the institution was only a side effect of voluntaryism. A preoccupation with the physical development of the institution without a corresponding appeal to the religious formation of the American Catholic community has indeed subsequently threatened the principle of voluntaryism.

England's ministry in Ireland and in the United States involved him in crucial questions about the external government of the church and its relationship to the state. (These questions, of course, troubled Catholics in Europe as well as in the United States.)[2] These issues, however, were fundamentally spiritual because they concerned the individual's internal religious convictions and the religious community's free public expression. By emphasizing the communal as well as the individual experience of religion, England and other Irish immigrants differed from many Enlightenment figures of the French and American Revolutions who reduced religion to the realm of the private. England's Enlightenment philosophy and his preoccupation with the questions of the external form of government preserved individual liberties without diminishing the spiritual nature of the religious community.

The fourth major contribution England and the Irish immigrants made to American Catholic consciousness was in the area of political philosophy. They demonstrated that Catholics were perfectly free to entertain their own political philosophies without in any way sacrificing Catholic teachings. They also showed that Catholics could be advocates of the political principles of republicanism without contradicting Catholic doctrines. In fact, the Irish immigrant bishop saw the contemporary world of republicanism, particularly the American style, as a place of opportunity, freedom and hope, and a place inherently friendly to the development of Catholicism. Such advocacy of republicanism provided an open door for Catholic entry into politics without creating conflicts with the church. The Irish Catholic tradition in this regard differed greatly from that of other Catholics' experiences with republicanism throughout the world.

England also helped to define American-Catholic identity by arguing that republicanism was inherent in Catholicism, that Catholicism was consistent with the political experiences of the American republic. In this regard, his diocesan constitution was convincing; but outside his own diocese republican practices were not a part of the contemporary American Catholic institutional experience. His articulations, therefore, reflected more his own vision for a new style of Catholicism than the concrete experience of most American Catholics.

Finally, England supported the development of the conciliar tradition and was the first Catholic to formulate a specifically American ecclesiology. England was not a systematic theologian either in Ireland or in the United States. He was, however, a creative pastoral theologian --i.e., he studied scripture, history, canon law, and theology in light of current political and religious experiences, and formulated theological responses to and pastoral programs for the specific needs of his day. His Enlightenment political philosophy and his democratic political experiences, influenced his reading of theological sources. His Irish experiences, in particular, enabled him to abstract a constitutional view of the church from his reading of Gallican ecclesiology. (The constitutionalism of medieval conciliar theology was most certainly the basis of much of the Gallican theology he read.) Referring to the church as a limited monarchy, applying his constitutionalism only to the relationship between the papacy and the episcopacy (the universal church and the national church), and excluding explicitly democratic elements, England thus created his own unique Galican theology of the church.

As an immigrant bishop, England adapted his earlier Galican theology to the American situation. Because of trusteeism and American republicanism, he applied his constitutional view to all levels

of the church -- from the congregational to the local diocesan, as well
as to the national and universal. Thus, American conditions extended
his constitutional view of the church.

American circumstances had other effects upon his ecclesiology. In
the United States, although he still saw the papacy as a limited monarchy, he no longer defined the church itself in terms of the papacy.
Rather than calling the church a limited monarchy, he referred to it as
a constitutional government. Likewise, he included democratic
elements in the government of the local church, and in his apologetical
writings he presented primitive and medieval ecclesiastical institutions
as forerunners of the democratic experience. He differed greatly,
however, from the trustees who had completely identified Catholicism
with American republicanism, and from his episcopal colleagues who
equated the church with the monarchic and aristocratic ecclesiastical
practices in Ireland and Europe; rather, England sought to accommodate Catholicism to republicanism in such a way as to preserve the
episcopal structure and simultaneously to protect republican participation. Not only American political institutions but also Protestant ecclesiastical practices encouraged England to formulate this kind of an
American ecclesiology. In fact, he saw Protestant constitutional
governments with their yearly conventions as consistent with the conciliar tradition of the ancient church. Thus, he perceived ecclesiastical
constitutionalism as part of the Catholic as well as American tradition.
The American experience, therefore, gradually transformed the nar-
rower constitutionalism of his Galican theology into the more comprehensive constitutionalism of his American ecclesiology.

In one area in particular American conditions seem to have had a
considerably conservative effect upon England's view of the church.
Although in Ireland he forcefully advocated domestic nomination, his
failure to support the cause in the United States was extremely inconsistent with his generally accommodating stance. The troubles of
trusteeism inhibited him. The more liberal bishops of the late nineteenth century and even the twentieth century episcopacy have been
reluctant to give the clergy more participation in the selection of the
bishops . The ghost of trusteeism still haunts American Catholicism.

Throughout his attempts to create an image of the Catholic Church
that would be American as well as Catholic, England did not use his
theological sources simply as proof texts to rationalize his own personal
experiences of the church and the age. England's theological
methodology was positive -- i.e., he took history and concrete experience into account in his theology, but, like the Gallicans, he was
not a critical-historical theologian. He either refused to admit certain

historical developments (e.g., the growth of papal power) or explained away those which did not fit into his constitutional perspective on the church. Thus, he used historical sources to reflect theologically upon his personal environment. In a way, without acknowledging it or perhaps even realizing it, he used his own personal environment as a source of revelation to interpret the Christian tradition. This approach to theology had one great benefit: it unwittingly broadened the scope of revelation and made the theological enterprise creative because it drew upon the political experiences of the world outside the church as a new source of revelation. On the one hand, such a creative theology served to translate the Christian experience in a new frame of reference (i.e., republicanism and constitutionalism) thereby making it more intelligible to the men of the day. On the other, it revealed that the bishop's role in the church was not only administrative and sacramental, but also interpretive -- i.e., the episcopal ministry demanded that the bishop research the theological sources in order to provide a Christian meaning for contemporary experience. This was pastoral theology: translating Christian life in terms of contemporary experience and interpreting contemporary experience in light of the Christian tradition.

The method also had its limitations. England's positive theological approach to pastoral problems made him consider his own proposals and programs to be in conformity with the Catholic tradition. His selective use of sources and his uncritical historical approach led him into an almost purely accommodationist stance in his American theology. Of course, these defects in methodology were common for Christian thinkers of his day. The weaknesses are inherent in any ecclesiastical situation where no critical theology exists, or where no dialogue or cooperation takes place between the more objective and systematic world of the theological schools and the more experiential world of ecclesial problems.

Although his theological method had inherent difficulties, his diocesan government which implemented his constitutional view of the church showed sound pastoral sensitivities. His creative adaptation of Catholic government to American republicanism emphasized both the democratic and monarchic aspects of Catholic republicanism. He stressed the central, but constitutionally limited, position of the episcopacy, the importance of a restricted clerical authority, subordination, and rational obedience, as well as the values of equality, election, collegiality, freedom, due process, and participation. The priest and the layman were thus the bishops' collaborators in this diocesan community; each had defined roles and responsibilities which mutually contributed to the upbuilding of the community.

Although he was successful in accommodating the church to American values in his own diocese, England was unproductive in the formation of the national church along similar lines. His repeated advocacy of a nationally-organized and uniformly-structured Catholic Church, however, eventually produced the Baltimore Councils. Such conciliar government was consistent with ancient Christian practices, American political institutions and Protestant polity. In specifics, however, the conciliar procedures developed along aristocratic, rather than republican or constitutional lines, as England had originally envisioned. The Baltimore Councils were primarily responsible for establishing a monarchical episcopacy at the local level and an episcopal aristocracy at the national level. Rather than providing for lay and clerical participation in the national government, the councils severly limited lay and clerical participation in all levels of ecclesiastical government. Thus, ironically, the councils destroyed England's constitutional vision of the church.

England did not succeed at the national level because many of his plans were closely linked to those of the trustees. His views were too optimistic, too republican, too liberal, and, in some minds, too Protestant for the bishops of his day. Although many of his ecclesiological emphases were consistent with the American temperament (and that of the Irish immigrants), they were not in accord with the dominant world-wide Catholic stress on the extension of ecclesiastical authority. His constitutional views of the limits of all church power did not fit the spirit of the times in the Catholic Church. He was a man ahead of his generation.

The development of a strong and exclusively monarchical episcopate, contrary as it was to England's vision, had its advantages for American Catholicism. Because episcopal power prevailed, the trustee schisms were healed; dissensions temporarily dissipated; clerical freedom from lay control was restored; and bishops assumed an advantageous position in the local communities enabling them to assist the phenomenal growth of the church and to fashion an immigrant Catholic unity during the mass immigrant invasion. The strong episcopal-centered church was also an effective instrument in creating a separate Catholic society within the United States to care for the social needs of the Catholic immigrants.

The development of an aristocratic episcopacy also had a corresponding number of disadvantages for nineteenth-century American Catholicism. The bishops' failure to acknowledge lay and clerical rights caused periodic discontent among the clergy and laity. The clergy rose up repeatedly to demand participation in diocesan decision-making and in the selection of bishops. The laity intermittently called for more accountability and lay responsibility in the church's life and government. The bishops' refusal to incorporate these elements of republicanism into the church's government, moreover, substantiated many American Protestant and nativist accusations that the Catholic Church was intrinsically incompatible with American republicanism. Thus, tensions and conflicts similar to the trustee and nativist period continued to appear in American Catholicism throughout the nineteenth and twentieth centuries. In fact, some of the dissensions in contemporary Catholicism are a reflection and a result of the suppressed conflicts of the early nineteenth-century. They represent the failure of the Catholic Church to resolve the ideological and practical conflicts between Catholicism and republicanism.

In view of the success of England's constitution and his theological approach to American society, one can conclude that the advantages occasioned by the development of a monarchical episcopacy might have been obtained without the corresponding disadvantages had the early nineteenth-century church adopted England's approach. Despite a difference in milieu, the issues in American Catholicism of the 1980s are analogous to those in the 1820s, and the conflicts of republicanism and Catholicism remain unresolved in the structures of ecclesiastical government. With some modifications England's constitutionalism, therefore, still represents a viable option for contemporary American Catholicism.

NOTES

section I

[1]Good historical treatments of the effects of the penal system can be found in Wall 1961; Brady and Corish 1971. A less nuanced view is presented by Lecky 1972.

[2]For the particular effects of the code upon ecclesiastical structures, see pp. 27-30. The laws had a partial effect in hindering the institutional and religious development of Irish Catholicism, but they could not succeed entirely in destroying it because the British did not have sufficient means to suppress all that the laws proscribed: they did not know the Irish language or customs; they were divided among themselves; they ruled local areas by absentee landlords. The English were, in a word, too far removed from Irish life to carry out the intended force of their system. See R.E. Burns 1962: 151. See also Lecky 1871: 129.

[3]Wall 1961: 13. The enforcement of these laws "at any given time depended on political rather than on religious considerations." See also Brady and Corish 1972: 3.

[4]The lay-clerical relationship was not always one of unanimity and peace. On this see pp. 28-30.

[5]On the effects of the French Revolution in England, see Vidler 1961: 34f.; and M. O'Connell May, 1956: 326f. O'Connell and Vidler agree that the English viewed the Catholic Church as a favorable force for conservatism after the Revolution. On John England's view of the beneficial effect of the French Revolution on Irish Catholic freedoms, see *Works, I, 193-94.*

[6]On O'Leary see, T. England 1822; Buckley 1868; Guilday 1924: 530-45. John England gave his brother Thomas many of the manuscripts which were used to write England's *Life of O'Leary*. John knew O'Leary's works, accepted much of his thinking on religious liberty and frequently quoted him in his own works. For O'Leary's influence on John England and other Irish Americans see Gorman 1939: 58, n. 25.

[7]For England's family history, educational background and the general circumstances of the veto question see, Guilday 1927: I, 36-123. England's participation in the questions of the day was revealed in the *Cork Mercantile Chronicle* which he edited from June 15, 1813, until the end of 1818. Copies of the newspaper are in the National Library, Dublin and the Cork City Library, Cork. England also edited a periodical called *The Religious Repertory*, see p. 35, in the years 1809, 1814 and 1815. The periodical contains much of the history of England's involvement in the religious and political reforms of the day. England, moreover, edited a prayer book, see p. 180, n. 49, for the renewal of religious life in Cork; and he published a number of texts for the revival of elementary education in Cork, see p. 180-1, n. 58. The history of the reforms in Cork will be told principally from these sources which I uncovered in Ireland in 1974.

[8]O'Connell's leadership in this movement seems unquestionable; see Coldrick 1974: 50-51, 136; Lecky 1871: 228; Beckett 1966: 247. Most general histories of the Catholic Church, except for J. MacCaffrey 1909, give O'Connell only a passing reference. O'Connell merits a place beside Chateaubriand, Lamennais and Lacordaire -- to name only a few of the Catholic spokesmen during the period who usually receive extended coverage in studies of Catholicism during the nineteenth century. His influence on Irish Catholicism, and thereby on Catholicism in the United States, also merits closer scrutiny. He has been given extended coverage in this study because of his close relationship with England and because of the similarity of their ideas. When England was about to leave Ireland for the United States in 1820, O'Connell gave him a "great dinner." See M. O'Connell 1972-77: II, 276. While England was Bishop of Charleston he wrote to O'Connell saying, "'scribble a few lines to an expatriated Bishop who was once your fellow-agitator and your ghostly father." *Ibid.*, 511. England acknowledged periodically that he had received his knowledge of law from O'Connell, see *Works*, III, 479.

[9]On Moylan see, O'Farrell 1973. John England and Moylan were close friends and associates even though they were separated by age and

ideas. Moylan did not appreciate clerical involvement in politics. England's political agitation, however, "raised no opposition from his bishop." *Ibid.*, 171. Moylan respected England's abilities, appointed him to a number of responsible positions in the diocese and made him the executor and sole administrator of his will. See *CMC*, Sept. 20, 1815.

[10]Nov. 30, Dec. 5, 12, 16, 21, 1808. The letters were signed by Fidelis, Powers' pen name.

[11]On the *Repertory* and religious reform, see p. 179, n. 48 and pp. 35-36

[12]*CMC*, March 17, 1810; cf. also Ward 1911-12: I, 141-57. Ryan's sermon was an embarrassment to Bishop Moylan; Moylan felt that Ryan had overstepped his competence as a priest in preaching on political questions. In 1816, Ryan reversed himself and attacked the tactics of the anti-vetoists in Dublin because of their clerical and lay interferences in religious matters which belonged to the bishops' domain.

[13]*CMC*, Jan. 1, 1812. The anti-vetoists and vetoists in Cork had their own organs of public opinion. *The Freeholder*, May 20, 1813, was a strong emancipation paper owned by a Catholic; it had supported the veto measure. *The Cork Advertiser and Commercial Register*, Jan. 12, 1813, and *The Southern Reporter*, May 21, 1818, were Protestant-owned papers which favored Catholic emancipation if the veto measures were attached to the bill. These last two papers had two things in common: they favored the veto and they opposed the "biased productions" of the *CMC*.

[14]Whyte 1960: 240, maintained that the clergy first participated in elections in 1826 in Waterford. England's participation in politics at this early date is at least one exception to Whyte's belief. In 1832, England recalled this adventure into politics by saying: "When I first appeared on the political arena, it was at a period, when all things looked loweringly for my country; and when hope itself scarce dared to whisper of success. When I first approached political strife I was clothed in a garb, which, under ordinary circumstances, would make me avoid contention and leave strife far behind. But there was a character in the strife which forbade me to retire; there was an object in the struggle which embraced all I held dear upon earth; for was it not a struggle for my religious as well as political liberty: It was on an occasion when our city was threatened with the loss of one of its best representatives, one, almost the only honest man in the British house of Commons at the time, that I stepped forward to vindicate the character of the class to which I belonged and to rescue, as far as in me lay, the city of my birth from becoming a filthy borough." This speech was

delivered by England at a banquet honoring England and O'Connell; it was reported in *CMC*, Aug. 31, 1832, and reprinted in *USCM*, Oct. 27, 1832.

[15]For England's account of the trial, see *Works*, V, 132-37.

[16]The *Dublin Evening Post* called the *Chronicle* one of "the most respectable provincial prints in Ireland . . . which circulates as much as *The Patriot* and *The Dublin Journal* together;" quoted in *CMC*, May 24, 1813. By 1815, the *Chronicle* had increased its readership to such an extent that it had become the largest newspaper in Cork and therefore in the entire province of Munster. The "Reverend Editor," as England was called by his enemies, found it necessary in one of the aggregate meetings of 1815 to defend himself and the *Chronicle* against various charges. The newspaper was accused primarily of being the "political priest's" public agency for promoting the Catholic religion. England responded by stating the principles upon which he felt the paper rested: "The *Chronicle* knows no man's religion, is subject to no party, and is as free to censure the acts of Doctor Milner [a Catholic] as to praise those of the Bishop of Norwich [a Protestant], and whilst it can respect and love such a Protestant as Geo Lidwell, without approving of his duelling, it can feel otherwise towards such a Catholic as Lord Fingall, without denying that he is actuated by motives of prudence." *CMC*, Sept. 18, 1815.

[17]*CMC*, Sept. 21, 1814: ". . . and did I conceive myself right, I would stand alone."

[18]On the results of the various lay and clerical conferences see *Repertory*, II, 53-64; 70, 137; 201-207; 345-50; cf. also *CMC*, May 18, 20, 27, 1814.

[19]Extensive excerpts of the letter are given here. Letter in *Dublin Evening Post*, July 7, 1818.

[20]*The Southern Reporter*, May 21, 1818. Catholics at the *Chronicle* did not accept the accusation without criticizing the government-sponsored *Southern Reporter*. The *Chronicle* charged that those at the *Southern Reporter* were not truly concerned with the poor of the city or they would have "restored to the poor the sums wrung from their misery" to pay for the publication of their paper (quoted in *Southern Reporter*, May 23, 1818). I could find no other extant copies of *CMC* after March, 1818, except a few for the month of March, 1820; most of the information on England and Cork for the period after March, 1818, therefore, comes from the *Southern Reporter*.

[21]Whyte, 1960: 240, has maintained that the influence of the Irish priests in the 1818 elections "must have been purely marginal." John England's participation in the Cork elections of that year is at least one major exception to Whyte's judgment.

[22]When England returned to Ireland in 1832, the *Dublin Register* said of him: "... but before he crossed the Atlantic he was the first Irishman who proved the value of the incorruptible forty-shilling freeholders of Ireland, when in the year 1818 by his energy and exertions, he secured through their means the triumphant return of the Hon. Christopher Hely Hutchinson," quoted in *USCM*, Oct. 27, 1832, p. 134.

[23]*The Southern Reporter*, July 14, 1818; cf. also *Dublin Evening Post*, July 18, 1818. An article in the *Dublin Evening Post* criticized England's July 14, 1818, speeches because he opposed the election of Sir Nicholas Colthurst simply on the grounds that he had been Peel's personal friend. Speaking of England, the editor said: "These are your politicians, these are the men who would hoodwink and lead the People."

[24]On his way to Europe in 1841, England stopped at St. Mary's Catholic parish in Halifax, Nova Scotia. The parishioners (mostly Irish) gave a dinner in his honor, saluting him for his work in the emancipation campaign in Ireland. England responded to their remarks by saying: "I had the good fortune to be found in that band of pioneers which opened the path in which millions have since made such glorious progress." Quoted in *USCM*, June 18, 1841, p. 399. On England's view of the relationship between politics and religion in Ireland and of the "duty of all Irish Catholics, without distinction of sex, or age, or condition, to use their best efforts, in the case of a contest, for the representation of a city, or county or borough in Ireland, to sustain the advocate of their cause, who was also the martyr of their country," see *Works*, III, 265. In these comments, England was justifying the role nuns took in Irish political life in Ireland during the veto and emancipation days.

[25]*Cork Advertiser*, Feb. 25, 1819. Cork Protestants seem to have been more favorable to Catholic claims at this time than were their Bandon neighbors; they united themselves behind a number of petitions to Parliament seeking unqualified Catholic emancipation. See *Southern Reporter*, March 16, 1819.

[26]Larkin 1962: 294, has described the nature of nineteenth century Catholicism in a different way. He perceives two kinds of churches in Irish Catholic society: the Roman and the Irish Catholic Church.

[27]The present state of historical evidence in Ireland makes it difficult to characterize with any precision the conditions of Catholic parish life. Lack of permanent episcopal residences and the poverty of the church did not allow the early-nineteenth-century bishops the luxury of preserving many of their papers. Furthermore, many of the diocesan

archives in the ecclesiastical province of Cashel, except for the archdiocesan archives of Cashel at Thurles, are just beginning to be
organized. It will take years to organize and then analyze these
episcopal papers. For the time being, therefore, any judgments about
Irish Catholicism at the congregational level must be made from
secondary sources and a few of the original documents that have been
preserved in various local Irish libraries and archives. The description
of Irish Catholicism found in this study is taken primarily from a study
of the Province of Cashel, with special attention given to Cork. On the
resources for a study of Irish Catholicism during this period, see Larkin
1967: 852-84; Larkin 1972: 626.

[28]For such congregational quarrels, see Brady and Corish 1972: 27-
29; Wall 1961: 35, 38, 44-45, 67. The second decree of the 1817 Provincial Council of Tuam legislated against such cases in the following
words: "Statuimus, quod, si factio aut seditio oriatur in aliqua nostrae
hujus provinciae parochia, in favorem cujusvis sacerdotis factiosi
grati, contra sacerdotem ab Episcopo ad eamdem parochiam regen-
dam deputatum, sacerdos ille, in cujus favorem istiusmodi seditio
fuerit excitata, ad dictam parochiam pro illa vice possidendam, ar-
bitrio Ordinarii, inhabilis censeatur. Nec ab hac constitutione ex-
cipiendos esse volumus eos, qui, juris patronatus laici quaesito colore,
se fulciri putarent," *Acta et Decreta*, III, 761.

[29]Greed seems to have bothered the poor peasant more than
drunkenness and concubinage. See Murphy 1969: 241.

[30]See Eighth decree of 1817 Provincial Council of Tuam, *Acta et
Decreta*, III, 763. Cf. also *Statuta* 1813: 123; cf. also p. 55. See also,
Brady and Corish 1972: 55.

[31]While John England was pastor of Bandon, he was robbed of an
eighteenth-century chalice and a small sum of money. See *Southern
Reporter*, Feb. 12, 1818.

[32]*Southern Reporter*, Nov. 23, 1819. A priest in Limerick was murdered in his own parish in November of 1819. The murder drew a
pastoral letter from Bishop Charles Tuohy of Limerick condemning the
action and exhorting the parish clergy to courage in the face of this
kind of danger. The bishop called the murder "unprecedented in our
country; Catholic priests have been at all times and through all
changes revered and loved by their flocks." Even though there is some
truth in what the bishop wrote, historical facts would not seem to
justify the remark that the murder was "unprecedented," see R.E.
Burns 1962: *passim*. Although the uprisings show some of the anti-
clericalism of the Irish peasant, they do not reveal the entire story
about the Irish-Catholic clergy-laity relationship on the local parish

level. Since the penal days, many of the Irish clergy had lived among their people, suffered the common struggle for survival, endured even more penal disabilities than did the peasantry, and identified themselves with the weaknesses of the peasantry. The common sufferings, desires for freedom, and hatred of the English oppression united the priests and people in intimate bonds which endured through most of the nineteenth century. On the local parish level, therefore, the relationship between the clergy and the people was not one of constant lay hostility nor one of complete harmony, but rather at times harmonious and at other times hostile. From the penal days until the famine clerical influence upon the people ebbed and flowed. See Murphy 1965: 104.

[33]John England to Jeremiah Holland, pastor of Inchigella, June 9, 1817 (Cork County Archives).

[34]Rome objected repeatedly to the Irish practice of saying that a candidate had been "elected" for the bishopric. See Whyte 1962: 15.

[35]Delahogue 1797: 187. Delahogue wrote his work on St. Cyprian shortly after reaching England after the outbreak of the French Revolution. The work was an argument against the positions taken by the bishops of the French constitutional church. He felt that these bishops had falsely interpreted Cyprian's treatise "On the Unity of the Church," and that they had especially misrepresented Cyprian's statements on the necessity of obtaining the testimony (temoignage) and election (suffrage) of the people in the selection of bishops. He felt that they had abused those texts in order to justify their own nominations. Ibid., 183. He compared the churches of the constitutional bishops to the schismatic African churches of Novatian and Fortunatus. Ibid., viii. According to England, Delahogue's theological tracts were used in many of the Irish, English, American, and French seminaries in the early nineteenth century. See USCM, Aug. 11, 1827: 42-43.

[36]CMC, June 24, 1814. At another time England disapproved "in toto" of a "system of the suffragans imposing a bishop upon a vacant diocese." See CMC, Aug. 29, 1817. Another priest, James Filan, opposed this type of nomination because it "stands condemned by the constant practice of the Church in all ages, at least down to the middle of the eighteenth century." All other practices which had developed in Ireland and elsewhere he believed to be contrary to the Catholic tradition. See, CMC, Aug. 6, 1817.

[37]On the historical, canonical, and theological reasons for the establishment of Deans and Chapters in a diocese, see articles by "Patricius" in CMC, Nov. 27, 29; Dec. 4, 1816; Aug. 6, 15; Sept. 10, 1817.

[38]See p. 177, n. 37.

[39]*CMC*, Nov. 29, 1816. Following Anacletus Reiffenstuel's *Jus Canonicum Universale*, Vitus Pichler's *Summa Juris Canonici*, and Lucio Ferrarius' *Bibliotheca*, Patricius maintained that the prelate could not act validly in a certain class of cases without the consensus of his chapter, nor in other cases could he act licitly without the chapter's counsel. See *CMC*, Dec. 4, 1816. England approved most of Patricius' proposals, but he thought the author overrated the chapter's authority. On Dec. 4, 1816, England wrote in *CMC*: "We are free to acknowledge, that in many of the acts regarding the chapter itself, and the regulation of its benefices, the consent of that Body is required, but not for those acts which are peculiarly of Episcopal authority, and necessary for the government of the diocese." England thought Patricius did not sufficiently acknowledge the bishop's rights and authority within the chapter. He believed that one could not properly promote the re-establishment of the chapter by overrating its authority and power.

[40]Bishop Charles Tuohy of Limerick made proposals similar to those of Patricius, see *CMC*, Aug. 20, 1817.

[41]*CMC*, May 20, 1814; Aug. 17, 1817. Bishop William Coppinger of Cloyne and Ross encouraged his clergy to submit proposals on the reform of nominating bishops.

[42]England and Doyle were the same age, were ordained bishops at about the same time, shared an active ministry in Ireland, and held parallel views of the church and politics. See *Works*, III, 511. In 1832, the students of St. Patrick's College at Carlow told England and Doyle that both bishops had "imbibed the same holy seeds of political truth and revealed wisdom" which motivated their political and religious conduct. See *USCM*, Nov. 17, 1832: 159. Most of Doyle's works on politics and religion were written after England left Ireland; they deserve a place in this study, however, because they articulate part of the new-breed Irish mentality to which England and many of the American Irish belonged.

[43]On the quinquennial synods, see *Southern Reporter*, Sept. 14, 1819. The Cashel Provincial Councils were legislative; see, *Statuta*. The enactments of the 1808 provincial synod were not sent to Rome for approval nor did they appear in the *Acta et Decreta*; the only Irish provincial council to appear in the *Acta* was the 1817 Provincial Council of Tuam, pp. 761-68. Why the Provincial decrees of Cashel did not appear in the *Acta* is not clear. Possibly the Irish bishops decided not to have Rome approve their enactments since the pope was imprisoned at the time or, perhaps, the strained relationship between Rome and Ireland at the time may have created an independent spirit among the

Irish bishops, who believed themselves to be the rightful administrators, overseers and legislators for their own churches. Whatever the reason may have been, the bishops did hold what they called "provincial councils" and they did enact laws for the churches of their province.

⁴⁴*Statuta*, 123f. The provincial bishops continued this meeting in August 23, 1808 at Cork. *Ibid.*, 129f.

⁴⁵*Ibid.*, 4: "Unde merito a Patribus Concilii Provincialis Coloniensis Synodi dicuntur *Corporis Ecclesiae nervi*, neglectus enim, ut aiunt, Synodis, non aliter Ecclesiasticus ordo diffluit, quam si corpus humanorum nervis solvatur."

⁴⁶See Walsh 1959 on the influence of the Presentations. Other sources on the religious reform in Cork are limited. The Cork diocesan archives have only a few documents from this period; the Cork library was completely destroyed by fire during the 1920's and the present library has few documents pertaining to the period.

⁴⁷On England's work in the area of social reform, see *CMC*, Sept. 26, Oct. 8, 1810; May 31, 1811; Dec. 8, March 5, 1813.

⁴⁸Eight issues appeared in 1809 and were collected in the *Repertory*, I, in 1810. The only copy of the book which I could find was in St. Patrick's College Library, Carlow, Ireland. Two issues of the periodical appeared in 1810, but no copies were discovered; eight issues were published in 1814, and were collected into a book the same year, see p. 172, n. 7. Four copies of this book were uncovered: one in the National Library, Dublin; one in each of the personal libraries of Fathers T.J. Walsh of Cork and Patrick O'Sullivan of the Killiney Franciscan House of Studies; one in the British Museum. At least four issues of the periodical were printed in 1815; three (for January, February, and March) were found in the library of St. Patrick's College, Maynooth; the fourth issue, advertised in the July 7, 1815 issue of *CMC*, was not discovered. Since no advertisements appeared in the *CMC* after July 7, 1815, one can conclude that England ceased to publish the periodical after that date. Guilday 1917: I, 83, called the publication *The Religious Repository*, as did Foik 1930: 76-77. Guilday was not able to find England's publications in preparing his life of England. The *Repertory* was printed anonymously but from internal and external evidence it is undoubtedly England's. Many of the stories which appeared in the *USCM* were originally printed in the *Repertory*, cf. *Repertory*, III, 49 and *USCM*, Oct. 16, 1822: 155; the style is also similar to England's; many of the articles England wrote for the *CMC* were later printed in the *Repertory*. In 1843, a year after England's death, Windele 1843: 142, attributed the periodical to

England. So also have others. See, Comerford 1886: I, 174; cf. also the *Dublin Catholic Directory* for 1843 quoted in *Works*, I, 2. A catalogue of Bishop John Murphy's library books (found in the Cork County Archives) also listed the *Repertory* under works written by England, see pp. 30 and 288. Murphy was bishop of Cork from 1815 to 1843.

⁴⁹In an attempt to revive the religious life of the people of Cork, England also edited a prayer book entitled "The Christian's Companion." According to an advertisement, *CMC*, Sept. 30, 1814, the work contained an exposition of Christian doctrine, appropriate prayers for several occasions, reflections on confession and communion, a number of examinations of conscience, a devotion to the Sacred Heart, and other private and liturgical prayers and spiritual exercises. A search through numerous libraries and archives in Ireland did not uncover the work.

⁵⁰On Carlow, where John England received his clerical education, see MacSuibhne 1943: 230-48. On Maynooth, see Healy 1895 and M. O'Connell 1956: 325-34, 406-15; 1957: 1-16.

⁵¹Doyle Letters 1824: 4; cf. also Fitzpatrick 1862: I, 350; McNamee 1969: 52. On Paley and his influence, see Storr 1913: 59.

⁵²A Maynooth student in a letter to the editor of *USCM*, Oct. 26, 1825: 263. The old Frenchman seems to have been Delahogue.

⁵³See, *infra*, Section II, p. 187, n. 22.

⁵⁴England was the presiding officer of a group of persons who called themselves "The Subscribers and Friends of the Poor Schools." The society collected funds; sought new methods of education; and held frequent meetings to inform the membership of the progress of their programs in Cork, to discuss various proposals for improving the system of education they were using, and to account for the way the funds were administered in the system. It was primarily, but not exclusively, composed of Catholic laity. On the society, see Corcoran 1928: 84.

⁵⁵*CMC*, July 19, 1815. England also instituted this sytem of education in Charleston. It was built upon the principles of religious freedom. See *USCM*, Aug. 14, 1822: 87.

⁵⁶England's speech before a meeting of the diocesan education committee in 1815. Quoted in Corcoran 1928: 85.

⁵⁷*CMC*, April 29, 1816. O'Connell and a number of Catholic bishops in Ireland proposed similar programs for education of the poor in Ireland. See, *CMC*, March 6, 1820.

⁵⁸England published two volumes of the *Rudiments*. No copy of this work was discovered; it was advertised in John England, *Reading Book* (4th ed.; London: John Murphy 1832: 1). The *Reading Book* was

probably first printed before Nov. 6, 1816, as is manifested from an advertisement in *CMC* on that date. Only the 1823 and 1832 editions were found; both of them were in the British Museum, London. In 1824, Bishop Doyle indicated that the book was "in general use throughout the several counties" of Wexford, Carlow, Queens and Kildare. See *USCM*, June 30, 1824; cf. also Brenan 1935: 435. Examinations before a committee of the House of Lords also indicated that the work was in general use in Ireland, see *Evidence* 1825: 32, 105.

[59]Other educational works have been attributed to England, but without evidence. A work called *Sketches of Irish History*, which was also widely used in Irish Catholic schools during the early nineteenth century has been attributed to England. See, Guilday 1927: I, 85, and Corcoran 1928: 24-25. The book was considered hostile to the British Government and some contemplated prosecuting the author. The book, however, was anonymous. England denied that he was the author and said it was written by an Ursuline nun, Sister Mary Ursula Young of Cork, see *Works*, III, 266. Even though the nun was the author, some have said that England certainly participated in writing the work. See Walsh 1959: 235. England was, at least, in basic sympathy with the work.

NOTES

---

section II

[1]*CMC*, April 19, 1816. On April 18 and 27, 1814, the *CMC* praised the restoration of the Bourbons because the new French constitution under the restored monarchy had recognized that a divergence in religious opinion should not cause a difference of political enjoyments. By 1815, however, the political climate had changed and so did the *CMC*'s evaluation of the Bourbon government. See *CMC*, Dec. 15, 1815: "We are far from justifying the men who would persecute anyone for conscience sake. We do not advocate the Inquisition, and we should deserve at least the penalty of the *lex talionis*, if we were wicked enough to approve of the barbarities at Nismes [*sic*], but we adhere to the assertion, that the Catholic subject of these realms, who is sent into exile, has less liberty of conscience than the man who is called a heretic in Spain or in Nismes [*sic*]."

[2]*CMC*, Sept. 5, 1814; see also O'Leary 1871: 345. For O'Leary, Jesus had furnished Christians "with no other means of making proselytes to his religion but persuasion, prayer and good example...the Kingdom of God is not of this world."

[3]*Repertory*, II, 33. Cf. also O'Leary 1871: 84; Doyle 1826: 205-206; McNamee 1969: 62. What Welch, 1972: I, 32, recently wrote about eighteenth-century theologians' positions on religious toleration can well be applied to England's thought: "Toleration did not mean for the important thinkers a commendation of indifference to religious questions, nor did it spring primarily from a judgement about human fallibility in matters capable of neither proof nor disproof; it was more

deeply a positive principle of freedom in faith and conscience springing from confidence in the possibilities of inquiry, from the morality demanded in rational inquiry, and from the hope for a more comprehensive awareness of God." P. Hughes 1929: 76f., has argued that "those [in Ireland and England] who fought for religious freedom for the Catholics saw the problem more from the political and practical perspective than they did from the perspective of principle." Although this judgment has some validity in general, it needs to be qualified in view of England's position. England's arguments for religious liberty were founded on his understanding of Christian principles. O'Connell's position was based on political rather than explicitly theological principles.

[4]Lecky 1972: 158. Subjection to legitimate political authority was a constant clerical theme in Ireland; see, Wall 1961: 64, 67, 68.

[5]On Bellarmine's views, see *Opera Omnia* 1856: I, 524-540; See also Murray 1948: 491-535. On the third Lateran decree, see Mansi 1759-98: XXII, 986-990 and Schroeder 1937: 242-244.

[6]Quoted in Gwynn 1928: 203; MacDonagh 1903: 93; cf. also Coldrick 1974: 212; on theology taught at Maynooth, see *USCM*, May 30, 1829: 372; on Doyle's position, see Fitzpatrick 1862: I, 403-404 and Doyle 1826: 11. Bishop Doyle taught that the popes' interventions in temporal affairs in the past "have done much mischief." In 1825, while discussing the possibility of the pope's involvement in Irish temporal affairs, Bishop Doyle told a British Parliament Committee: "if the popes were to intermeddle in the rights of the King, the priests would exercise all their powers, even their spiritual powers by preaching to the people and teaching them to oppose the Pope were he to do such a thing. The pope cannot interfere in political or civil affairs." See *Evidence* 1825: 348. When Doyle was faced with the opposition of Bellarmine, he responded: "When Bellarmine or Turrecremata are objected to us, why not allow us to prefer to them Ambrose, Chrysostom or Bossuet?" See Doyle 1826: 21; he also quoted from Irenaeus, Athenagoras, Justin, Theophilus of Alexander, Tertullian, St. Augustine, and various popes to show a Catholic tradition on the denial of the pope's political powers. Revealing his Gallicanism, Doyle asserted, furthermore, that even the pope's spiritual powers were limited in the church. "No Bull of any pope can decide our [Irish bishops] judgment, if it be not received and assented to by the pastors of the church." *Ibid.*, 37.

[7]O'Leary 1871: 330-331. The social compact theory of government was widely held in Ireland. According to Bishop Doyle, the rights of man "proceed from the social compact.... Social intercourse does not depend on the religious opinions of men; it is founded upon their man-

ners or morals, and subsists by their conduct; when their conduct is not in opposition to the laws of nature, or to the preservation and well-being of the state, their speculative religious opinions should never be taken cognizance of by the law." See, Doyle 1823: 47. Doyle periodically quoted Montesquieu, Locke and others to support his social compact theory of government and to uphold the separation of church and state. Cf. also Doyle 1825: 88, 237.

[8]J. O'Connell 1867: II, 16. On O'Connell's position on the separation of church and state, see Coldrick 1974: 168-169, 198. Coldrick maintained that O'Connell regarded the separation principle as "historical and relative, rather than as transcendent and self-justifying."

[9]J. O'Connell 1867: II, 28-34. Cardinal Consalvi respected the faith of these Irish Catholics but said that some of them did not hesitate to use "the pretext of religion to favor their political designs and purposes against the government they hate." See Ellis 1942: 96. Consalvi also felt -- probably because he favored a concordat between Rome and the British government -- that the Irish clergy were politically naive; they did not understand contemporary church-state relationship, and were thinking in terms of the church-state relationships of two or three centuries previous.

[10]Doyle 1825: 241. Doyle evidently did not advocate the absolute separation of church and state. He felt that "though its [the state's] union with one [i.e., religion] may, and perhaps should always continue, it cannot justly punish any religion which is not opposed to the public interests." Whether this position was motivated by principle or from expediency, i.e., from fear of the British reaction to an advocacy of absolute separation of church and state, is difficult to say. Doyle seems to have been arguing from principle, but proof of this would over-extend the present paper.

[11]Doyle 1826: 12; see also Doyle 1825: 241-42. Doyle frequently quoted from Prov. 8:15-16; Dan. 2:37; Rom. 13:1-2, 4; 1 Pt. 2:13; Jn. 18:36; Mt. 8:20; St. Bernard's De Consideratione, chapter 6, to show Christian support for the position he took on the source of the state's power and the relationship between state power and ecclesiastical government.

[12]CMC, Nov. 21, 1814. Speaking of O'Connell, England wrote in an editorial: "but we have seen him sometimes manifest an inclination to one weakness -- an amiable and generous one, perhaps, in private life --he is unsuspecting." England felt that O'Connell may have been willing to compromise somewhat on the veto question, to aid the movement for Catholic emancipation.

[13]Works, III, 476-520. In 1825, as a bishop in America, England

chided O'Connell for departing from the path of unqualified emancipation by agreeing to the possibility of the state payment of the clergy
as a condition for emancipation.

[14]*Repertory*, III, 18. In 1815, England printed an account of what he
called the "Catholic Question in America." At issue was a case decided
at the court of General Session in the city of New York on whether a
Catholic priest could be forced to disclose the secrets of auricular confession in a court trial. In reporting the court's decision, that the priest
could not be compelled to reveal confessional secrets, England wrote:
"When this adjudication shall be compared with the baneful statutes
and judgments in Europe, upon similar subjects, the superior equity
and wisdom of American jurisprudence and civil probity will be felt,
and it cannot fail to be well received by the enlightened and virtuous of
every community, and will constitute a document of history precious
and instructive to the present and future generations." England kept
abreast of American civil and religious happenings and frequently
reported them in the *CMC*. He reported the death of the "venerable"
Archbishop of Baltimore, John Carroll, *CMC*, March 11, 1816. He
printed the annual presidential addresses to congress and numerous
other items of political interest; periodically he held up American
republicanism for its superior wisdom, especially in the area of the
separation of church and state, see *CMC*, Feb. 13, 1818.

[15]*CMC*, Dec. 26. 1815. On England's view of the 1799 episcopal
decision, see *CMC*, Jan. 31, 1816.

[16]Anti-vetoists, like Daniel O'Connell and Bishop Doyle were not absolutely nor consistently against state pensions. Coldrick 1974: 188, n.
33; *Works*, III, 511. During the veto question, O'Connell protested the
pensioning of the clergy; in 1825, however, he agreed to the measure in
order to achieve emancipation; he later changed his mind and resisted
the measure when he realized that it was rejected by a majority of the
Irish spokesmen. After 1825, he remained unalterably opposed to state
payment. Doctor Doyle felt that pensioning the clergy should not be
considered a means for emancipation, but he did not condemn the
measure absolutely. See Doyle 1825: 291: "But if the Catholics were
emancipated a provision could be made for the Catholic clergy uncon-
nected with, and totally independent of court favour, and which
would not add probably a single shilling to the burthens of the
country."

[17]Sociological factors (as much as anything else) seem to have influenced the Irish Catholic's practice of voluntaryism. Murphy 1965:
104, has noted that the Irish system of church support was voluntary
"only in the sense that it had no legal basis of compulsion as had the

tithe system; otherwise, custom, necessity and community pressure ensured that it had a very real sanction in fact." In 1830, Felicite de Lamennais used the Irish historical experience of voluntaryism to support his call upon the French Catholic Church to initiate a similar system in France. See *USCM*, Dec. 11, 1830, p. 190.

[18]*CMC*, June 6, 1814. England and the anti-vetoists (and perhaps all oppressed Christian peoples) identified poverty and persecution with the religion of Jesus. They made frequent references to those passages in the scriptures and in Christian tradition that indicated that the religion of Jesus was not of this world, that Jesus "only promised persecution, and recommended poverty to his followers." *Repertory*, II, 181. England, however, overestimated the benefit of the *regium donum* to the Presbyterian clergymen; it most certainly did not provide them with a "life of comfort." See Beckett 1948: 106-115.

[19]*CMC*, Sept. 1, 1815. On Aug. 18, 1815, Bishop Moylan of Cork wrote to John England to commend England's gathering of the clergy of the diocese in opposition to the Quarantotti Rescript while Moylan was absent from the diocese. He was confident that whatever the clergy of the diocese decided in their confidence would be "for the Glory of God, and the welfare of *our national Church*." Letter printed in *CMC*, Aug. 18, 1815. In 1817, the Dublin Catholic Board, under O'Connell's leadership, issued a circular to the Catholic bishops objecting to Propaganda's involvement in the discipline of the Irish Church "as if this were a mere missionary country without a national church." Quoted in Coldrick 1974: 149.

[20]*Repertory*, II, 400-405. England relied on one of Peter Gandolphy's (1779-1821) controversial sermons for the comparison.

[21]*CMC*, Aug. 21, 1815. England's constitutional view of the church was used later in the United States. There, however, England compared the church's constitution to the American one and emphasized the democratic elements in the church. See pp. 119-127.

[22]On Tournelly's Gallicanism see, M. Dubruel 1095-1137; cf. also Yves Congar 1932, and Hocedez 1949: III, 93f. Tournelly, like many of the Gallicans, stressed the limitations of papal powers; for him, the popes were limited in the government of the church by the nature of the church itself and by its canons. Tournelly saw the pope more as a guardian of the tradition than as a source of the church's law. He used Gratian's collection of laws and St. Bernard's *De consideratione* to show that the pope ought to protect and respect the jurisdiction of each bishop. England also frequently quoted from *De consideratione*, e.g., *Repertory*, I, 64, 135-39; *CMC*, Aug. 30, 1815. Because they read Gallican sources, England and many of the early nineteenth century

Irish bishops and clergy have been repeatedly accused of being "Gallican." See, Y. Congar and R. Aubert in Nedoncelle 1960: 15, n.; 375; cf. also MacCaffrey 1909: II, 447; Rousseau 1969: 72; Nolan 1948: 13; Rome also suspected the Irish seminaries of Gallicanism in the early nineteenth century. See McNamee 1966: 59. The term "Gallicanism" has so many different connotations that it does not seem to be a useful tool for describing the kind of theology which developed in Ireland during this period. One thing is sure: political Gallicanism did not exist in Ireland after the Protestant Reformation, except for a short period in the late seventeenth century. See, Brennan 1957: 219-37; 283-309. Referring to the "brief interlude," Brennan noted, p. 219, "its promoters were infected by the current theological theory of Gallicanism, foreign as it might seem to the history and traditions of Irish Catholicism." Gallicanism was foreign to the Irish anti-vetoist's mentality. Although they used Gallican sources, they were not Gallicans. What they developed during this period was a Gaelic, rather than a Gallican, theology of the church which emphasized an independent communion with the Roman Church and articulated and adapted aspects of Gallican thinking to Irish circumstances.

[23]*CMC*, Aug. 21, 1815, quoting Tournelly, *De eccles*, II, 62. On the same point, England also quoted Bellarmine, *De Rom. Pont.* Cap. 5. Lib. 1.

[24]*CMC*, Aug. 21, 1815. England quoted Bossuet's *Sermon sur l'unite de l'Eglise* which presents the church as a "restrained Monarchy." England also used Cyrpian, Augustine and Pope Boniface I on the equality and unity of the episcopacy, and various church councils and papal letters to show that even though the pope had pre-eminence of jurisdiction and solicitude for the church, he nevertheless shared the episcopacy with the other bishops; thus, his powers were limited by the very nature of the church and the equality of the episcopacy. Cf. also *CMC*, March 29, 1816.

[25]*CMC*, Aug. 21, 1815, quoting Bellarmine, *De Rom. Pont.* lib. 4, c. 2. England called Bellarmine "an eternal advocate for Papal prerogatives. Our respected countryman, O'Leary, put him to sleep on the dust of the most obscure shelf of the Library, because he said he was mad for the extension of Papal power. I think we may awaken him now to assist us to restrain it."

[26]*CMC*, May 18, 1814. England is quoting the preface to the Ephesian canons rather than a particular canon. See Mansi 1901: IV, 1470.

[27]*CMC*, May 18, 1814. The passage quoted is not in Jerome's fifty-second letter. I could not discover the proper source of England's quotation. England frequently used those who most strongly favored

papal prerogatives -- like Jerome and Bellarmine -- to show that even they acknowledged constitutional limits. Cf. also *CMC*, Aug. 21, 1815.

[28]*CMC*, Aug. 21, 1815. On the strong reaction to these statements see Guilday 1927: I, 95, n. 18.

[29]*CMC*, March 15, 1815; cf. also *CMC*, April 17, 1815. England's apprehensions about Troy were apparently justified as one of Troy's letters reveal. After the Quarantotti Rescript, Troy wrote to Archbishop Thomas Bray of Cashel on May 5, 1814, saying: "Rescripta Roma venerunt. Causa finita est.... By the enclosed copy, your Grace will perceive that the *Veto* has been granted by the Holy See to His Majesty our Sovereign. Whatever be our sentiments on the subject, it is our duty to acquiesce in the decision of such authority and set an example of submission to it." Letter found in the Cashel Archdiocesan Archives "Bray Papers." Troy and a number of the other Irish bishops were Roman-trained and were considered Cisalpines. According to Ellis 1942: 87, Troy was not representative of the Irish hierarchy; a number of Irish bishops at the time, however, were willing to submit to Rome and to the British Government to obtain concessions from the government.

[30]The view of the Irish priest as a social or political reformer was not universally accepted. At the beginning of the nineteenth century, most priests in Ireland had very little to do with politics and temporal affairs. The dominant tradition of the Irish priests was one of nonresistance inherited from the France of the *ancien regime* where most of the clergy of the day had been trained. See Whyte 1960: 239. Some Catholic bishops even made a concerted effort to counsel priests "to avoid all political interferences as unworthy of the ministers of him whose kingdom is not of this world." See Hussey's 1796 Pastoral in *Repertory*, II, 488.

[31]Bishop Francis Moylan to Archbishop Thomas Bray, April 26, 1813, Cashel Archdiocesan Archives, "Bray Papers": "All the bishops must unite before it is too late to avoid Lay control or superintendence."

NOTES

section III

¹On the circumstances surrounding England's episcopal appointment, see Guilday 1927: I, 283-298; see also Hutch 1875: 514; Fitzpatrick 1862: II, 5.

²England's apologetics are found primarily in *Works* I-V and *USCM* (1822-1842).

³Encyclical printed in *USCM*, July 7, 1834: 386, with commentary which reveals that the editor is obviously embarrassed by the teaching.

⁴In Ireland, England had argued for religious liberty and against religious indifference. Religious liberty did not imply religious indifference, see pp. 50-51.

⁵*Works*, I, 107. England condemned previous Catholic intolerances, but said little about contemporary Catholic prejudices against Protestants.

⁶*Works*, I, 110. Discouraged with the existing organization of the Catholic Church in the United States before the Baltimore Councils, England indicated that individuals were responsible for Catholic apologetics since there was no national Catholic organization to do the work. "As we cannot assemble as a body to do this; as our Bishops do not find it convenient or expedient to act as the Irish Bishops and English Vicars have done under similar circumstances, an individual has taken the liberty of addressing to you his sentiments on the subject."

⁷*USCM*, July 17, 1830: 18; cf. also Feb. 25, 1832: 279; Sept. 5, 1840: 65f.

[8]See Rousseau 1969: 376, for a thorough analysis of England's American arguments on separation. Rousseau's otherwise-excellent study has one major flaw -- it does not present England's Irish position on separation and therefore does not expose the Irish roots of his American arguments. My examination here will not reproduce England's American arguments in detail since I have already exhibited substantially the same reasoning when I presented England's Irish position on separation. See pp. 58-62.

[9]*Works*, III, 511. Daniel O'Connell, unlike England, made no exception to the principle of separation. He asserted that even in the papal territory church and state should be separated. See M. O'Connell 1975: 182.

[10]*USCM*, June 7, 1834: 390. During the 1830's the *USCM* held Lamennais and Montalembert in high esteem, quoting from them periodically. After *Mirari Vos* and *Singulari Nos*, the *USCM* reported little about Lamennais. On December 13, 1834, p. 191, it mentioned that the pope had condemned Lamennais on June 25, 1833, but the encyclical condemning him was not printed, even though the usual policy was to publish all official documents from Rome. On February 21, 1833, p. 271, it announced that Montalembert submitted to the Roman encyclicals; on October 16, 1837, p. 123, it reported the rumor from France that Lamennais was preparing to recant his errors. The *USCM* expressed the hope that he would return to the Catholic Church. After this period, nothing appeared in the newspaper on Lamennais.

[11]Handlin 1951: 126, has noted that most immigrants found the voluntary practices of all religious institutions in the United States "unfamiliar and disturbing." This was not the case with the Irish-Catholic immigrant.

[12]*Works*, V, 55. The Scotch-Irish Presbyterians, unlike the Irish Catholics, had a difficult time adjusting to the circumstances of voluntaryism in the United States. See, Trinterud 1949: 204: "The Scotch-Irish had never been accustomed to paying their clergy a regular salary. Most of the Presbyterian ministers of Ulster lived almost entirely upon Royal Bounty."

[13]*Works*, III, 506; cf. also Papers Relating 1897: 305-08. Bishop F. P. Kenrick was more critical than England of the possible corruptions of the clergy because of clerical poverty. See, Kenrick's 1836 Letter on Church Union printed in O'Shea 1904: 236: "I am also sensible that the dignity of religion is compromised when the poverty of its ministers leaves them in a state of mendicity or dependence."

[14]*De Romano Pontifice*, Chp. III, lib. 1, quoted in *USCM*, Jan. 28, 1824: 52.

[15]*Works*, V, 149. Most Irish Catholics, England believed, were enthusiastic republicans. One of the arguments against giving emancipation to the Irish Catholics, he maintained, was the English accusation that the Irish were "Republicans in principle." See *USCM*, Jan. 21, 1824: 35.

[16]According to Murtha 1965: 175, Maréchal objected to England's frequent use of words such as "democracy, liberalism, and tyranny, as well as the emphasis on democratic rights in the *Miscellany*." The "hyperliberalism" of the lay trustees, Marechal felt, had warped their respect for ecclesiastical authority. He believed that England's advocacy of republicanism was not compatible with a respect for ecclesiastical authority.

England realized that this republicanism irritated some of his episcopal brethren. He saw their hostility to republicanism as a result of the French Revolution, see *Works*, IV, 33. He described the French in this country as: "Nearly ignorant of our language, scarcely recovered from the terrors of the atrocities with which their infatuated and infuriated countrymen had disgraced the name of liberty, and smarting under the wounds inflicted upon them in the name of republicanism...." American Protestants, like the American bishops, found England's championship of republicanism incompatible with his adherence to Catholicism. England discovered the source of Native American antipathy to Catholicism in Protestant history books which misrepresented Catholics on the question of republicanism. On August 25, 1823, he wrote to William Gaston, "Upon the first charge -- Hatred of Republics -- I have been obliged to go again and again over Hume's History and Essays, Gibbon's works, Hallem's Middle Ages and Sismondi's History of the Italian Republics besides a number of sidelong references -- to Burnet, Mosheim and others.... I am now convinced from what I have thus read, and conversing with many of our *literati* here, that it is only by rectifying the gross misrepresentations of history the prejudices of America can be encroached upon," in Letters 1907: 387. Writing to Daniel O'Connell on October 4, 1823, he indicated again that the Catholic Church had been misrepresented in most English histories, especially Hume's, and that his primary task was to show the Americans where their histories had misrepresented the Catholics, in M. O'Connell 1972: II, 510-11. Cf. also *Works*, III, 499.

[17]Although England supported Félicité de Lamennais' principles of religious liberty and voluntaryism, he did not agree with his earlier ideas on government. Lamennais 1895: 212 considered the social contract theory of government to be "pure atheism." He was, of course,

referring to Rousseau's theory. He believed that the social compact "only establishes a conflict of arbitrary wills and by destroying the notion of right and duty or the principle of obedience, it constitutes a state of war between the authorities and subjects." *Ibid.*, p. 190. England was aware of Lamennais' *Essay*, see *USCM*, Feb. 18, 1824: 105.

[18]In the following section, pp. 131-139, the Catholic part of the constitutional government will be considered.

[19]For a history of the constitution, yearly conventions and opposition to the "democratic" form of government, see Guilday 1927: I, 343-80, II, 480-502.

[20]Constitutional forms of government were popular for all religious and civil societies at the time in Charleston. The Protestant Episcopal Church in the United States had a general constitution for the government of the church on the national level and a local state constitution for the state level. The form of government in each case was similar to that of the federal constitution because many who participated in the formation of the church governments had previously taken part in the formation of the national constitution. See, Albright 1964: 16; cf. also, *Journal of the Proceedings* 1829: I, 40-44. The *Journal* is found in the Archives of General Theological Seminary Library, New York, New York. The Presbyterians and the Baptists, likewise, had their national and state constitutions to guide them in their government. The Baptists were working on a state constitution for their associations in South Carolina in 1821. On December 4, 1821, they opened their first convention in Columbia, South Carolina. The need to unite to aid foreign missions and to provide education was the primary impetus behind the Baptist constitutional movement in South Carolina. See, King 1964: 181; cf. also Maring and Hudson 1963: 171. England did not lack sources for examples of ecclesiastical government based upon the constitution of the United States. He studied the numerous Protestant constitutions and confessions of faith and quoted from them repeatedly in his apologetical writings. See, *Works*, I, 180-90; 216-18; 219, 224, 226, 227. The great similarity between his constitution and that of the Protestant Episcopal Church of South Carolina was no accident. He had believed in Ireland that the government of the Church of England and that of the Catholic Church were similar. It is no wonder, then, that he imitated much of the Protestant Episcopal government in this country. Even the yearly episcopal addresses to the convention delegates followed the same pattern of those of Bishop Nathaniel Bowen of the Charlestown Episcopal Church. See *Journal of the Proceedings* 1829.

England was a decided constitutionalist; his diocesan constitution was one of many he framed. As early as 1822, he had already formed a constitution for a society in his diocese for the dissemination of books of piety and instruction. See. *The Laity's Directory* 1822: 116-20. Almost every society he established in his diocese had its own constitution. He wrote, for example, the constitution for the Order of the Sisters of Mercy, an order of Religious women he founded in his diocese; he constructed a constitution for the Society of Christian Doctrine in Savannah, Georgia, see *USCM*, March 24, 1824: 191; he helped the episcopal Bishop Nathaniel Bowen form a constitution for the Charleston Anti-Duelling Association, which he and Bowen established in Charleston, see *USCM*, Oct. 7, 1826: 94; he formed a constitution for the Society Friendly to St. Mary's Church, a society created to help defray expenses for the building and operation of the church, see *USCM*, Aug. 3, 1839: 38. He also followed the example of many Protestant groups by forming a constitution for the Roman Catholic Missionary Society, to help spread the gospel in his own missionary diocese, see *USCM*, Jan. 24, 1835; cf. also *Works*, IV, 435. He likewise instituted a constitution for the Brotherhood of St. Marino, a society (or as England called it, "a republic") of working men organized for the purposes of developing mutual support in the practice of economic industry and practical religion, see *USCM*, Aug. 25, 1838: 62-63.

[21]*Works*, V, 92. In a letter to Archbishop Marechal, Bishop Conwell objected to England's statement that the bishop had his jurisdictional powers "by divine right *immediate* as successor to the apostles." Conwell to Marechal, June, 1824, in Archives of the American Catholic Historical Society of Philadelphia. Conwell said that this was not a matter of faith because others held a different opinion, especially in Rome. He believed that the Apostolic See was the proper channel of ecclesiastical jurisdiction.   England's view of the divine right of the episcopacy and the implications of that perception are treated in Section IV.

[22]On October 8, 1964, Bishop Stephen Leven of San Antonio, Texas, called upon the bishops at the Second Vatican Council to study England's constitution as an effective instrument for lay participation in the church. See *Council Daybook* 1965: III, 117; cited in Kaib 1968: iv.

[23]*Works,* IV, 230; many of England's ideas on the relationship between Catholicism and republicanism were similar to Rene Francis Augustus Chateaubriand's ideas. England read and frequently quoted from the *Genius of Christianity*. On the nature of representation and the Catholic Church, see Chateaubriand 1856: 662: "To the glory of

our religion be it also said that the system of representation partly originated in the ecclesiastical institutions; for the Church exhibited the first model of it in her councils, composed of the sovereign pontiff, the prelates, and the deputies of the inferior clergy; and then the Christian priests, not having separated themselves from the state, gave rise to that new order of citizens which by its union with the two others completed the representation of the political body."

[24]*Works*, IV, 205-06. England's republican enthusiasm led him to exaggerate the extent of republicanism in the church; all religious orders were not built upon republican principles. He never mentions, for example, the structure of the Jesuits.

[25]Bishop F.P. Kenrick 1850: 155 quite wrongly saw "that the representative system [of the constitution] was adopted in a way to satisfy the cravings of a few for distinction, and yet to make them weary of the trouble and formality." The laity responded with enthusiasm to England's convention system as numerous letters and petitions to England reveal. The letters and petitions can be found printed in the *USCM* every year in November after the yearly conventions. The laity, at least, were not wearied by the system.

[26]*Works*, IV, 223; cf. also *USCM*, Jan. 28, 1824: 55. England believed that there was no more perfect Republican Constitution than that of St. Dominic.

[27]England's call for the re-establishment of cathedral chapters in Ireland revealed that he was sympathetic to a body of episcopal counsellors. The cathedral chapter provided a number of constitutional limits upon episcopal power besides giving the canons some rights and some voice in protecting the rights of the whole diocese. In spite of the obvious differences between the constitution and the chapters, enough similarities, particularly the general idea of defining and limiting all rights and duties within the diocese, suggest that England may have had the idea of a cathedral chapter in mind when he created his diocesan constitution. The fact that he never formed an actual cathedral chapter after energetically advocating its re-establishment in Ireland is further evidence that the constitution may have substituted for the chapter. In the first constitution in the United States, furthermore, he used a vocabulary similar to chapter terminology. He defined, for example, the "Vicar Capitular's" rights in the diocese during the vacancy of the Episcopal See. See, *The Laity's Directory* 1822: 117, 119. Even though England never participated in the deliberations of any existing chapters, he was aware of the constitutional nature and purpose of chapters. See *supra*, pp. 32-34. On the constitutional provisions of chapters in the Middle Ages, see Burns 1962: 14-23; Torqueblau: 530-95.

[28]See Letter of England to Conwell, March 3, 1824, printed in Guilday 1927: I, 361: "The great evil has arisen from having built and recognized churches upon vague and indistinct terms instead of having a detailed constitution from which there would be no departure."

[29]*Works*, IV, 417; cf. also III, 243: Papers Relating 1897: 316: Referring to the constitution, England wrote in 1836, "The general principle is that the duties of the clergy ought to be regulated by the bishop: and that the people shall support them while they discharge those duties to the satisfaction of the prelate; and that in the mode of raising and expending money for church purposes, everything shall be done by the common consent of the clergy and of the principal laymen under the bishop's direction. And that in all cases of difference the bishop's decision shall be final, unless it be disapproved upon complaint to the Holy See."

[30]England believed that priests had not received due recognition since the establishment of the American hierarchy. They were many times subjected to the personal whims of their bishops or the laity. "They have only delegated jurisdiction which can be taken from them at the pleasure of the bishops, and has frequently been so taken, without any chance for appeal." See, Papers Relating 1897: 461. England hoped the constitution would be one vehicle for appeal beyond excessive local episcopal control. Cf. also *Works*, V, 227.

[31]Before the establishment of the diocesan constitution, England found that some clergy had unlimited power and authority in their parishes. See, *Works*, III, 243: Priests forgot "the boundary of their sphere and endeavored to encroach upon that of the laity." Cf. also *USCM*, Oct. 26, 1825: 261.

[32]*Works*, V, 107. England repeatedly called for a national council of bishops. One of his purposes for such efforts was to limit what he considered to be the arbitrary use of episcopal power. On that point see, pp. 149-160.

NOTES

section IV

[1]*Works*, IV, 199; cf. also II, 292. England's concept of the church was a mixture of theological and political principles. England, like many of the conciliarists of the fifteenth century, used the image of the body of Christ as the theological basis of his constitutional view of power and authority in the church. On the conciliarists, see Jacob 1953: 3, 11-12.

[2]Yves Congar in Nedoncelle 1960: 90, has shown that most nineteenth-century Catholic theologians stressed the church as a perfect society. They emphasized almost exclusively the question of ecclesiastical authority, especially its precise nucleus.

[3]*Works*, I, 195-96. England failed to note a major difference between the two forms of government. The three powers of governing in the Catholic Church were not as specifically separated into different branches of government as they were in the United States. The pope as well as the bishops were at the same time legislators, judges and executives. England frequently used this legal terminology to describe the nature of the church. For him, the entire church was the living witness to God's revelation. *Ibid.*, I, 135; II, 176: "God is the legislator in religion; the church is his witness, the authority emanates from God alone, the testimony from the Church." See *Ibid.*, II, 293-94. God established an authentic tribunal of judges, the universal body of bishops, within the church for ascertaining and judging the truth of revelation. *Ibid.*, I, 64; II, 48-49. In deciding between divergent views of truth the bishops were to apply the "common rules of evidence."

"That rule is: examine the witnesses fully as to the fact, and if the vast majority, under proper circumstances will agree in the testimony, it is the evidence of truth." See, *Ibid.*, IV, 182. The witnesses were scripture, tradition, ecclesiastical laws, customs, and the living testimony of the members of the church. England frequently compared the Catholic Church's manner of discovering and defining truth and of establishing authority to the American judicial procedures which were used for similar purposes.

[4]*Works*, IV, 230. F.P. Kenrick believed that in such comments England was responding to the "popular prejudice against the church." Kenrick stated that England's comments were merely "oratorical flourish" rather than his true views on the nature of church government. He felt that England's zeal to meet the prejudices of the day led him into "some exaggeration." Kenrick responded: "for in sober truth we cannot affirm that the institutions of the Church are purely republican. The illustrious prelate, on other occasions, distinctly stated that they combine the advantages of each form of government, without the usual evils attendant upon them…. The Church, we have heard him say in a discourse before the provincial council, has the energy of monarchy, without its absolute character; the wisdom of enlightened aristocracy, without the incubus of hereditary nobility; the equality of a republic, without the fluctuation of popular caprice." See Kenrick 1850: 150. Kenrick identified "republicanism" with pure democracy, whereas England associated the term with a mixed form of government.

[5]The medieval conciliarists, as well as England, "thought that the church was a polity, a mixed government, not a unitary absolutism; that the Popes were subject to natural and divine law, and that the papal power could be both curtailed and regulated by periodical assemblies of Western Christendom…. [the conciliarists] had a view of history which enabled them to justify their theories by precedents drawn from earlier periods in the life of the church." See Jacob 1953: 2.

[6]*Works*, II, 285, quoting Bellarmine, *De Conciliorum Authoritate*, Book II, chap. 14. Bellarmine asserted that this was a position held by a large number of orthodox Catholics, including Jean Gerson.

[7]*Works*, I, 57-58. F.P. Kenrick believed England's thought limited the powers of the church excessively. "Since the Constitution [of the United States] leaves religious sentiment free, and interferes in no way with the exercise of Church authority, we need not labor to circumscribe it, in order to satisfy the prejudices of individuals." See Kenrick 1850: 147. According to Kenrick, the American separation of

church and state allowed the Catholics in the United States an opportunity to develop their appreciation for ecclesiastical and papal
authority. For England, that separation implied that the limits of
power within the church should be as carefully defined as those within
the state. Kenrick's view that separation provided an opportunity to
develop and extend ecclesiastical authority and England's perception
of separation as the occasion to limit that authority constitute two
classical American Catholic interpretations of the implications of
separation.

[8]*Works*, V, 92. F.P. Kenrick did not agree with England's comparison of the pope to the president, nor of the council to the Congress.
See Kenrick 1850: 147: "The Pontiff, according to the definition made
in the Council of Florence, has full power of governing the universal
church; which plenitude of power cannot be ascribed to the President
in reference to the Union or to the governor of a State." Cf. Nolan
1948: 45.

[9]*Works*, V, 96. F.P. Kenrick asserted that England's constitutional
denial of papal infallibility was "improper"; he felt that such a formal
declaration was a major blemish in the constitution. See Kenrick 1850:
143; cf. also Guilday 1927: I, 367-68.

[10]*Works*, I, 321. F.P. Kenrick disagreed repeatedly with England's
attempts to define and limit papal powers. See Kenrick 1850: 146: "It
did not please the Divine Founder of the Church to give her a written
constitution, by which the powers of her rulers should be defined. He
chose one among his apostles to be his special representative and
viceregent, to whom he gave a plenitude of authority in the most express terms, and under symbols the most significant. No limits to its exercise are assigned; but those which arise from right, justice, and the
general good are essentially implied." Kenrick's Roman ecclesiastical
training put him squarely on the side of the ultramontanists. England's
Irish education put him in the camp of the episcopalists, i.e., those who
favored the rights of the national churches. Both Kenrick and England
were Irish immigrants; their differences on this point can be explained
by their dissimilar educational backgrounds. Much more study remains
to be done on the divergent theologies in nineteenth-century American
Catholicism.

[11]See William Read's evaluation in *Works*, I, 17; cf. also, Kenrick
1850: 157; Guilday 1927: II, 68-111; Guilday 1932: 96; Greeley
1967:89-92.

[12]During the first Baltimore Council a *USCM* reporter underlined
the geographical catholicity of the meeting. Writing from Baltimore he
reported: "We have here seven Prelates from five nations: three natives

of the United States, one of France, one of Ireland, one of England, and one of Italy; this is really a specimen of Catholicity." See, *USCM*, Oct. 10, 1829: 118. To put down rumors of the Irish-French tension in the American Church, the same reporter noted that Bishop Flaget, a Frenchman, chose Francis Kenrick, an Irishman, as his theologian; likewise Bishop England chose Simon Brute, a Frenchman, as his theologian.

[13]*USCM*, Nov. 2, 1833: 142. On seventeenth and eighteenth-century Irish provincial councils and diocesan synods, see Brady and Corish 1971: 31-32.

[14]James Whitfield to Nicholas Wiseman, June 6, 1833, in English College Archives, Rome, Microfilm Archives, University of Notre Dame quoted in McAvoy 1969: 130; cf. also Matthew Panczyk 1963: 66; Papers Relating 1897: 18; Guilday 1927: I, 532.

[15]Billington 1964: 37-38. A priest, writing in the *USCM* during the first council, predicted that the Protestant reaction to the councils would be one of fear. He forewarned that the "Cant-Gospellers" would see nothing but horror and increase of "Popery" in the assembly of bishops. He noted, furthermore, that the Protestants would accuse Catholics of Inquisition, despotism, Jesuitism, and that this would all happen "whilst hundreds of Episcopalian, Presbyterian, Methodist or other Ministers might assemble without exciting alarm or regard." *USCM*, Oct. 24, 1829: 125. Archbishop Whitfield feared the Protestant reaction and preferred holding no more councils after 1829. He favored a low profile for Catholicism in the United States. In 1831, he wrote to England indicating his predisposition for no future councils because they would only be injurious to Catholicism. "For my part I am quite adverse to unnecessary agitation and excitement; experience seems to prove, that walking silently in the steps of my predecessor, doing what good Providence puts in our way and publishing it as little as possible has with God's blessings promoted Religion more and made it more respectable in the eyes of Protestants than if a noisy stirring course had been pursued." Whitfield to England, Dec. 27, 1831 in AAB; cf. also Panczyk 1963: 50-51. England's evaluation of the practical relationship between the American Catholic Church and Protestantism was diametrically opposed to that of most American bishops.

[16]England to Whitfield, Jan. 4, 1832 in AAB; cf. also *USCM*, Jan. 28, 1832: 242; June 9, 1832: 398; England to Whitfield, June 13, 1832 in AAB; in 1832, England went to Rome, among other reasons, to use his influence there to force Whitfield to call a second council. While in Rome he wrote his brother-in-law, Michael Barry, in Cork on May 9, 1833, saying: "I am likely to secure the administration of the church of

the United States upon a plan which I trust will be very useful and almost all my views will be concurred in"; letter in the Archives of the Franciscan House of Studies, Killiney, Ireland.

[17]By 1840, England felt that he had been a total failure in the provincial meetings. All of his favorite projects and proposals were rejected by his fellow bishops. England to Samuel Eccleston, Feb. 7, 1840 in AAB. Kenrick told Paul Cullen that the American bishops had no reason to fear England since "their votes could always outweigh his arguments"; Kenrick to Cullen, Mar., 1834, Papers Relating 1897: 18; cf. also Guilday 1927: I, 532.

[18]On this, see Carey 1975: 243, n. 51. On the development of episcopal legislation and the influence of American legal tradition on episcopal perceptions of lay participation in the church, see Fogarty 1972: 83-105.

[19]USCM, Oct. 18, 1828: 112: "One of the first benefits which we could expect from the American Synod, would be the devising of some plan by which the zeal of the people might aid the wisdom of the Bishops in providing ministry for our province." Cf. also USCM, Nov. 22, 1828: 153. Prior to the first Baltimore Council, England wrote to Archbishop Whitfield, Dec. 25, 1828, in AAB, suggesting that the laity should be called upon for their aid in the education of priests and that their cooperation on this project should be discussed at the coming council.

[20]According to F.Kenrick 1850: 157, many feared England and his influence upon the national church because they felt that his proposals if they gained acceptance "would occasion agitation among the clergy and people, and lead to rash innovations. The ardent character of the Bishop of Charleston was not calculated to diminish this apprehension."

[21]More recently, LeBuffe 1973: 147, made similar accusations. "The historian might remark that England's system of Church governance seems more American and Congregational than Catholic -- an example of High Federalist Republicanism in Catholic Church polity during an age of growing democracy -- a belated surfacing of a curious Euro-American hybrid." Such a judgment does not understand England's Catholic collegial view of the Church.

[22]England to Rosati, Jan. 14, 1833, in Rothensteiner 1927: 270; cf. also Works, V, 422; Albright 1964: 14, has shown that the constitution and laws of the Protestant Episcopal church in the United States were based upon conciliar procedures. The "legal structure [of the Protestant Episcopal Church] is specifically based upon the Canon Law of the Church of England and both in its canons and its constitution it has

preserved the dependence upon continuous conciliar procedure and the intention to abide by the purpose of the historical church of which it is a part."

[23]This analysis is based upon a report of the first annual diocesan convention. See *USCM*, March, 1824: 178-79. The report contains England's ideas on the signficance of the conventions.

[24]*Works*, IV, 384. In 1826, in an address to the Georgia convention, England acknowledged the fear of some of the Catholics in the South to express their faith: "You are equally as well aware as I am of the reluctance which exists in the minds of many Roman Catholics to make what they consider a useless profession of their faith in places where not only are our tenets and principles altogether misunderstood, but where we are most grossly misrepresented by men who are supposed to know us, but who if they are not very ignorant must be worse than ignorant."

[25]1829 Pastoral of American Hierarchy to Priests, in Guilday 1923: 47. The American pastorals until 1840 were written by England.

[26]On Marechal's views, see Marechal 1819 and Carey 1975: 259-60. Cf. also Kenrick 1843: 21, who agreed with England and Marechal on this point -- as did most of the American hierarchy at the time.

[27]*Works*, V, 154. England's rejection of the laity's right to elect bishops was consistent with the position he had taken in the veto controversy in Ireland. In 1834 and 1837, however, while serving as an Apostolic delegate to Haiti, England felt forced to concede to the President of Haiti the right to nominate episcopal candidates. He did this in order to arrange a concordat between the papacy and the Haitian government. He was convinced that the participation of the laity in the selection of bishops was historically unjustified, but he felt forced to concede the right in Haiti in the hope of preserving religion there. On the Haitian affair, see Rousseau 1973: 269-88.

[28]England to Whitfield, May 14, 1833, in AAB. In the *USCM*, England periodically reported the election of bishops to Irish Sees, most of which were by the priests of a vacant diocese or by chapters. See, *USCM*, June 21, 1834: 407. England, however, never publicly stressed the rights of priests to elect their bishops in the United States. In the *USCM*, he periodically commented upon the inadequate way in which bishops were selected in the country, but he never argued for clergy participation in that selection process. See *USCM*, April 12, 1834: 326; April 19, 1834: 234.

[29]During the First Baltimore Council, England advocated, without success, the establishment of canonical parishes in the United States to give the clergy canonical rights in the American Church. See Casey 1957: 59-60.

[30]Letter of Rev. Joseph Stokes to Daniel O'Connell, April 29, 1825, printed in M. O'Connell 1972- : III, 157.

[31]What Albright 1964: 17, has said of the incorporation of the laity into the government of the Protestant Episcopal Church in the United States could be applied with some justice to the Charleston diocesan government. "The introduction of laymen into the government of the church was hardly an innovation, but rather the restoration of a very ancient principle in conciliar history." What Albright said of William White, Protestant Episcopal Bishop of Philadelphia, could be applied with some qualifications to England's reasons for inviting the laity into the church's government. *Ibid.*, p. 18: White felt that the "laity might more easily be brought to accept the ecclesiastical laws of the church if they had a share in their development." England of course wanted to secure the laity's support for diocesan regulations but he realized that the laity were not permitted to participate in the formation of all ecclesiastical legislation. He did, however, give them a voice in matters of jurisdiction relating to the temporalities of the church; in doing this he granted much of what the trustees had sought from church authorities.

[32]Circular letter from the Lay Delegates of the 1826 South Carolina Convention "To the members of the Church of South Carolina and to their brethren in the States of Georgia and North Carolina." Nov. 11, 1826, printed in *USCM*, Nov. 18, 1826: 138.

[33]*Works*, II, 241. England's denial of the laity's right to choose their own pastors was inconsistent with his attempt to relate the Catholic Church to republican principles and practices. He rejected the practice, however, because of the evil consequences which followed it.

NOTES

---

conclusions

[1]The minority status of the Catholic bishops and their fear of nativists' charges also seem to have influenced the episcopal failure. England's generally accommodating stance toward American society is partially responsible for his failure in this area.

[2]On problems in English Catholicism, see Bossy 1975: 295-390.

bibliography

archives

Archives of the American Catholic Historical Society of Philadephia,
   St. Charles Borromeo Seminary, Overbrook, Pennsylvania.
Baltimore Archdiocesan Archives, Baltimore, Maryland.
Cashel Archdiocesan Archives, Thurles, Ireland.
Charleston Diocesan Archives, Charleston, South Carolina.
Cork County Library Archives, Cork, Ireland.
Cork Diocesan Archives, Cork, Ireland.
English College Archives, Notre Dame, Indiana.
Franciscan Archives, Franciscan House of Studies, Killiney, Ireland.
Kerry Diocesan Archives, Killarney, Ireland.
Notre Dame University Archives, Notre Dame, Indiana.
Philadelphia Archdiocesan Archives, Philadelphia, Pennsylvania.
The Sacred Congregation de Propaganda Fide Archives, on microfilm,
   Notre Dame, Indiana.

newspapers

Cork Advertiser and Commercial Register.
Cork Mercantile Chronicle.
Dublin Evening Post.
Dublin Review.
The Freeholder (Cork).
The Southern Reporter (Cork).
United States Catholic Miscellany (Charleston, South Carolina).

separate works

Acta et Decreta Sacrorum Conciliorum Recentiorum Collectio Lacensis. 7 Vols. Freiburg: Herder, 1870-1886.

Adams, W.F. Ireland and Irish Emigration to the New World from 1815 to the Famine. New Haven: Yale University Press, 1932.

Ahlstrom, Sidney E. A Religious History of the American People. New Haven: Yale University Press, 1973.

Albright, Raymond W. "Conciliarism in Anglicanism." Church History, XXXIII (1964), 1-30.

Beckett, J.C. Protestant Dissent in Ireland 1687-1780. Vol. II: Studies in Irish History. Edited by T.W. Moody, R.D. Edwards and B.B. Quinn. London: Faber and Faber, Ltd, 1948.
The Making of Modern Ireland, 1603-1923. London: Faber and Faber, Ltd., 1966.

Billington, Ray A. The Protestant Crusade, 1800-1860. Chicago: Quadrangle Paperbooks, 1964.

Black, Anthony. Monarchy and Community: Political Ideas in the Later Conciliar Controversy, 1430-1450. Cambridge: Cambridge University Press, 1970.

Bolster, Evelyn. "The Moylan Correspondance in Bishop's House, Killarney: Part I," Collectanea Hibernica, XIV (1971), 82-142.

Bossy, John. The English Catholic Community, 1570-1870. London: Oxford University Press, 1976.

Brady, John and Corish, Patrick J. The Church under the Penal Code. Vol. IV, No. 2: A History of Irish Catholicism. Dublin, Ireland: Gill and Macmillan, 1971.

Brenan, M.J. An Ecclesiastical History of Ireland from the Introduction of Christianity into that Country, to the Year 1829. Rev. ed. Dublin: James Duffy, 1864.

Brenan, Martin. Schools of Kildare and Leighlin, A.D. 1775-1835. Dublin: M.H. Gill & Son, Ltd., 1935.

Brennan, James. "A Gallican Interlude in Ireland," The Irish Theological Quarterly, XXIV (July, Oct., 1957), 219-37; 283-309.

Buckley, M.B. The Life and Writings of the Rev. Arthur O'Leary. Dublin: James Duffy, 1868.

Burke, William P. The Irish Priests in the Penal Times (1660-1760). Introduction by Patrick Corish. Reprint of 1914 edition. Shannon, Ireland: Irish University Press, 1969.

Burns, Richard I. "The Organization of a Mediaeval Cathedral Community: The Chapter of Valencia (1238-1280)," Church History, XXXI (1962), 14-23.

Burns, Robert E. "Parson, Priests and the People: The Rise of Irish Anti-Clericalism, 1785-89," *Church History*, XXXI (1962), 151-163.

Carey, Patrick. "John England and Irish American Catholicism, 1815-1842: A Study of Conflict." Unpublished Ph.D. dissertation, Fordham University, 1975.

"Two Episcopal Views of Lay-Clerical Conflicts: 1785-1860." *Records of the American Catholic Historical Society of Philadelphia*, LXXXVII (March-December, 1976), 85-98.

Casey, Thomas F. *The Sacred Congregation de Propaganda Fide and The Revision of the First Provincial Council of Baltimore (1829-1830). Analecta Gregoriana, LXXXVIII Series Facultatis Historiae Ecclesiastiae*. Rome: Gregorian University Press, 1957.

Chateaubriand, Rene F.A. *The Genius of Christianity*. Trans. Charles White, 2nd. rev. ed. Baltimore: John Murphy & Co., 1856.

Coldrick, Helen. "Daniel O'Connell and Religious Freedom." Unpublished Ph.D. dissertation, Fordham University, 1974.

Concilia Provincialia Baltimori habita ab anno 1829 usque ad annum 1849. Baltimore, 1853.

Comerford, Michael. *Collections Relating to the Dioceses of Kildare and Leighlin*. 3 Vols. Dublin: James Duffy and Sons, 1886.

Congar, Yves. "Gallicanisme," *Catholicisme*. Edited by G. Jacquemet. 7 vols. Paris: Letouzey and Ane, 1947-77. IV, 1731-39.

Corcoran, Timothy. *Education Systems in Ireland from the Close of the Middle Ages*. Louvain: H. Bomans, 1928.

Corish, Patrick J. *The Origins of Catholic Nationalism*, Vol. III, No. 1, *A History of Irish Catholicism*, edited by P.J. Corish, Dublin: Gill and Son, 1968.

Council Daybook Vatican II, Session 3. Edited by Floyd Anderson. Washington, D.C.: National Catholic Welfare Conference, 1965.

Curtis, Edmund. *A History of Ireland*. 6th ed. rev. London: 1960.

Delahogue, Louis A. *Saint Cyprien*. London: W. and C. Spilsbury, 1791.

Tractatus de Ecclesia Christi. 5th ed. Dublin: John M. O'Toole, 1848.

"Diary of Archbishop Marechal, 1818-1825," *Records of the American Catholic Historical Society*, XI (1900), 417-451.

"Diurnal of the Right Rev. John England, First Bishop of Charleston, South Carolina, 1820-1823," *Records of the American Catholic Historical Society*, VI (1895), 29-55; 184-224.

Doyle, James W. *A Vindication of the Religious and Civil Principles of the Irish Catholics.* Dublin: Richard Coyne, 1823.
  A Defense of His Vindication of the Religious and Civil Principles of the Irish Catholics. Dublin: Richard Coyne, 1824.
  Letters on a Re-union of the Churches of England and Rome from and to the Rt. Rev. Dr. Doyle, R.C. Bishop of Kildare, John O'Driscol, Alexander Know and Thomas Newenham. Dublin, Ireland: Richard Moore Tims, 1824.
  Letters on the State of Ireland. Dublin: Richard Coyne, 1825.
  An Essay on the Catholic Claims. Dublin: Richard Coyne, 1826.
Dubruel, M. "Gallicanisme," *Dictionnaire de theologie catholique.* Edited by A. Vacant and E. Manquenot. 15 vols. Paris: Letouzey and Ane, 1903-50. VI Part 2, 1095-1137.
Ellis, John T. *Cardinal Consalvi and Anglo-Papal Relations, 1814-24.* Washington, D.C.: Catholic University of America Press, 1942.
  American Catholicism. Chicago: The University of Chicago Press, 1955.
  ed. *Documents of American Catholic History.* Milwaukee: The Bruce Publishing Co., 1962
[England, John.] *The Religious Repertory.* Cork: J. Haly Publisher, 1810.
  The Religious Repertory. Cork: Charles Dillon, 1814.
  The Religious Repertory. Nos. 19-21 (January, February, March, 1815).
  Reading Book, Containing Useful and Pleasing Lessons, with an abridgement of a Considerable Portion of Sacred History. 3rd ed. London: John Murphy, 1823.
England, Thomas. *Life of the Rev. Arthur O'Leary.* London: Longman, Hurst, Rees, Orme, Brown, and Keating, Brown and Co., 1822.
The Evidence taken before the Select Committees of the Houses of Lords and Commons appointed in the Session of 1824 and 1825 to inquire into the State of Ireland. London: John Murray, 1825.
Fitzpatrick, William J. *The Life, Times, and Correspondence of the Right Rev. Dr. Doyle.* 2 Vols. Boston: Patrick Donahoe, 1862.
Fogarty, Gerald P. "Church Councils in the United States and American Legal Institutions," *Annuarium Historiae Conciliorum,* IV (1972), 83-105.
Foik, Paul J. *Pioneer Catholic Journalism.* United States Catholic Historical Society Monograph Series XI. New York: The United States Catholic Historical Society, 1930.

Giblin, Cathaldus, O.F.M. *Irish Exiles in Catholic Europe*. Vol. IV,
  No. 3: *A History of Irish Catholicism*. Edited by Patrick
  J. Corish. Dublin: Gill and Macmillan, 1971.
Gleason, Philip, ed. *Catholicism in America*. New York: Harper
  and Row Publishers, 1970.
Gorman, Robert. *Catholic Apologetical Literature in the United States
  (1784-1858)*. Vol. XXVIII: *Studies in American Church
  History*. Edited by Peter Guilday. Washington, D.C.:
  The Catholic University of America Press, 1939.
Grant, Dorothy. *John England, American Christopher*. Milwaukee:
  Bruce Publishing Co., 1949.
Greeley, Andrew M. *The Catholic Experience: An Interpretation
  of the History of American Catholicism*. New York:
  Doubleday and Co., 1967.
Griffin, Martin I.J. "The Story of St. Mary's," *American Catholic
  Historical Researches*, X (1893), 2-16; 50-74.
  "The Life of Bishop Conwell," *Records of the American
  Catholic Historical Society*,XXIV (1913), 16-42; 162-178;
  217-250; 348-361; XXV (1914), 52-67; 146-178; 217-248;
  296-341; XXVI (1915), 64-77; 131-165; 227-249; XXVII
  (1916), 74-87; 145-160; 275-283; 359-378; XXVIII
  (1917), 64-84; 150-183, 244-265; 310-347; XXIX (1918)
  170-182; 250-261; 360-384.
Guilday, Peter, ed. *The National Pastorals of the American Hierarchy
  (1792-1919)*. Washington, D.C.: National Catholic Wel-
  fare Council, 1923.
  The Catholic Church in Virginia (1815-1822). United
  States Catholic Historical Society Monograph, Series
  VIII. New York: The United States Catholic Historical
  Society, 1924.
  "Arthur O'Leary," *Catholic Historical Review* IX (1924),
  530-45.
  The Life and Times of John England. 2 Vols. New York:
  The America Press, 1927.
  "John England, Catholic Champion," *Historical Records
  and Studies*, XVIII (1928), 171-195.
  "Trusteeism," *Historical Records and Studies*, XVIII
  (1928), 7-73.
  A History of the Councils of Baltimore (1791-1884).
  New York: The MacMillan Co., 1932.
Gwynn, Denis. *The Struggle for Catholic Emancipation, 1750-1829*.
  New York: Longmans, Green and Co., 1928.

Hales, E. E. Y. *Revolution and Papacy 1769-1846*. Garden City, New
    York: Hanover House, 1960
Handlin, Oscar. *The Uprooted: The Epic Story of the Great Migra-
    tion that Made the American People*. Boston: Little,
    Brown and Co., 1951.
Hassard, John R. *Life of the Most Reverend John Hughes, First Arch-
    bishop of New York*. New York: D. Appleton and Co.,
    1866.
Healy, John. *Maynooth College: Its Centenary History*. Dublin:
    Browne and Nolan, Ltd. 1895.
Hennesey, James. "Papacy and Episcopacy in Eighteenth and Nine-
    teenth Century American Catholic Thought," *Records
    of the American Catholic Historical Society*, LXXVII
    (1966), 175-189.
Hocedez, Edgar. *Histoire de la Theologie au XIX Siecle*. 3 Vols. Paris:
    Desclee de Brouwer, 1949.
Hopkins, Thomas. *St. Mary's Church, Charleston, S. Carolina*.
    Charleston: Presses of Walker, Evans and Cogswell,
    1898.
Hudson, Winthrop S. *The Great Tradition of the American
    Churches*. New York: Harper Torchbooks, 1963.
Hughes, Emmet John. *The Church and the Liberal Society*. Prince-
    ton, New Jersey: Princeton University Press, 1944.
Hughes, John. *Controversy Between Rev. Messrs. Hughes and Breck-
    enridge, on the Subject "Is the Protestant Religion the
    Religion of Christ?"*. Philadelphia: Isaac Bird, 1833.
    and Breckinridge, J. *A Discussion of the Question, Is the
    Roman Catholic Religion in any or in all its Principles or
    Doctrines, Inimical to Civil or Religious Liberty. . . .*
    Philadelphia: Carey, Lea and Blanchard, 1836.
Hughes, Philip. *The Catholic Question, 1688-1829*. London: Sheed
    and Ward, 1929.
Hutch, William. *Nano Nagle: Her Life, Her Labours and Their
    Fruits*. Dublin: McGlashow & Gill, 1875.
Inglis, Brian. "O'Connell and the Irish Press, 1800-42," *Irish Histor-
    ical Studies*, VIII (March, 1952), 1-27.
Jacob, E. F. *Essays in the Conciliar Epoch*. 2nd ed. Manchester:
    Manchester University Press, 1953.
Kaib, Virginia Lee. "The Ecclesiology of John England, The First
    Bishop of Charleston, South Carolina 1821-1842." Un-
    published Ph. D. dissertation, Marquette University,
    1968.

Kehoe, Lawrence, ed. *Complete Works of Bishop John Hughes; Comprising his sermons, letters, lectures, speeches, etc.* 2 Vols. New York: L. Kehoe, 1865.

Kenneally, Finbar. *United States Documents in the Propaganda Fide Archives.* 7 Vols. Washington, D. C.: Academy of American Franciscan History, 1966- .

Kenrick, Francis P. *A Review of the Second Letter and Postscript of the Right Rev. John Henry Hopkins, D.D.* Philadelphia: M. Fithian, 1843.

[Kenrick, Francis P.] "Bishop England's Works," *Brownson's Quarterly Review*, IV (April, 1850), 137-159.

King, Joseph M. *A History of South Carolina Baptists.* Columbia, South Carolina: R. L. Bryan Co., 1964.

The Laity's Directory. Revised and corrected by the Rev. John Power. New York: William H. Creagh, 1822.

Lamennais, Felicite de. *Essay on Indifference in matters of Religion.* Trans. Lord Stanley of Alderley. London: John MacQueen, 1895.

Larkin, Emmet. "Church and State in Ireland in the Nineteenth Century," *Church History*, XXXI (1962), 295-306.

"Economic Growth, Capital Investment, and the Roman Catholic Church in Nineteenth Century Ireland," *American Historical Review*, LXXII (April, 1967), 885-905.

"The Devotional Revolution in Ireland, 1850-75," *American Historical Review*, LXXVII (1972), 625-652.

The Roman Catholic Church and the Creation of the Modern Irish State, 1878-1886. Philadelphia: The American Philosophical Society, 1975.

Latourette, Kenneth S. *The Nineteenth Century in Europe: Background and the Roman Catholic Phase.* Vol. I: *Christianity in a Revolutionary Age: A History of Christianity in the Nineteenth and Twentieth Centuries,* 5 Vols., New York: Harper and Brothers, 1958-1962.

LeBuffe, Leon A. "Tensions in American Catholicism, 1820-1870: An Intellectual History." Unpublished Ph.D. dissertation, Catholic University of America, 1973.

Lecky, William E. *The Leader of Public Opinion in Ireland: Swift, Flood, Grattan, O'Connell.* London: Longmans, Green, and Co., 1871.

A History of Ireland in the Eighteenth Century. Abridged with an introduction by L. P. Curtis. Chicago: The University of Chicago Press, 1972.

Leflon, Jean. *La Crise Revolutionnaire 1789-1846*. Vol. XX: *Histoire de l'eglise* 21 Vols. Edited by Augustine Fliche and Victor Martin. Paris: Bloud and Gay, 1934-1952.

"Letters from the Right Reverend John England, D.D., to the Honorable William Gaston, LL. D. 1821-1829." *Records of the American Catholic Historical Society*, XVIII (1907), 367-388; XIX (1910), 98-140.

MacCaffrey, James. *History of the Catholic Church in the Nineteenth Century*. 2 Vols. Dublin: M. H. Gill and Son, Ltd., 1909.

MacDonagh, Michael. *Bishop Doyle "J.K.L.," A Bibliographical and Historical Study*. London: P. F. Unwin, 1896.

Daniel O'Connell and the Story of Catholic Emancipation. London: Burns Oates and Washbourne, Ltd., 1903.

MacSuibhne, Patrick. "The Early History of Carlow College," *Irish Ecclesiastical Record*, 5th Series, LXII (Oct. 1943), 230-48.

Mansi, J. D., Martin, J. B., and Petit, L., eds. *Sacrorum conciliorum nova et amplissima collectio* 53 vols. Paris: H. Welter, 1901-27.

Marechal, Ambrose. *Pastoral Letter to the Roman Catholics of Norfolk*. n.p., 1819.

Maring, Norman H. and Hudson, Winthrop S. *A Baptist Manual of Polity and Practice*. Chicago: The Judson Press, 1963.

Maynard, Theodore. *The Story of American Catholicism*. New York: The Macmillan Co., 1941.

McAvoy, Thomas. "The Formation of the American Catholic Minority, 1820-1860," *The Review of Politics*, X (Jan., 1948), 13-34.

"The Catholic Minority in the United States, 1789-1821," *Historical Records and Studies*, XXXIX-XL (1952), 33-50.

A History of the Catholic Church in the United States. Notre Dame: University of Notre Dame Press, 1969.

McCaffrey, Lawrence J. "Irish Nationalism and Irish Catholicism: A Study in Cultural Identity," *Church History*, XLII (Dec., 1973), 524-534.

McCarthy, Charles. "The Historical Development of Episcopal Nominations in the Catholic Church of the United States (1784-1884)," *Records of the American Catholic Historical Society*, XXXVIII (1927), 297-354.

McDougall, Donald J. "George III, Pitt, and the Irish Catholics, 1801-1805," *Catholic Historical Review*, XXXI (Oct., 1945), 255-81.

McElrone, Hugh P., ed. *The Choice Works of the Right Reverend John England, Bishop of Charleston, South Carolina*. 2 Vols. Baltimore: 1884.

McManners, John. *The French Revolution and the Church*. Vol. IV: *Church History Outlines*. Edited by V. H. Green. London: SPCK, 1969.

McNamee, Brian. "The 'Second Reformation' in Ireland," *The Irish Theological Quarterly*, XXXIII (1966), 39-64.

"J. K. L.'s Letter on the Union of Churches," *The Irish Theological Quarterly*, XXXVI (1969), 46-69.

Messmer, Sebastian G., ed. *The Works of the Right Reverend John England, First Bishop of Charleston*. 7 Vols. Cleveland, 1908.

Moody, Joseph N., ed. *Church and Society: Catholic Social Thought and Political Movements, 1789-1950*. New York: Arts, Inc., 1953.

Mooney, Canice. *The First Impact of the Reformation*. Vol. III, No. 2: *A History of Irish Catholicism*. Dublin: Gill and Son, 1967.

Murphy, John A. "The Support of the Catholic Clergy in Ireland, 1750-1850," *Historical Studies*, V (1965), 103-121.

"Priests and People in Modern Irish History," *Christus Rex*, XXIII (Oct., 1969), 235-260.

Murray, John C. "St. Robert Bellarmine of the Indirect Power," *Theological Studies*, IX (1948), 491-535.

Murtha, Ronin J. "The Life of the Most Reverend Ambrose Marechal, Third Archbishop of Baltimore 1768-1828." Unpublished Ph.D. dissertation, Catholic University of America, 1965.

Nedoncelle, Maurice, ed. *L'Ecclesiologie au XIXe Siecle*. Vol. XXXIV: *Unam Sanctam*. Paris: Les Editions du Cerf, 1960.

Niebuhr, Helmut R. and Williams, Daniel D., eds. *The Ministry in Historical Perspective*. New York: Harper and Row Publishers, 1956.

Nolan, Hugh J. *The Most Reverend Francis Patrick Kenrick, Third Bishop of Philadelphia, 1830-1851*. Vol. XXXVII of *The Catholic University of America Studies in American Church History*. Washington, D. C.: Catholic University of America Press, 1948.

Nuesse, Celestine J. *The Social Thought of American Catholics
    1634-1829.* Washington, D. C.: Catholic University of
    America Press, 1945.
O'Brien, Joseph L. *John England—Bishop of Charleston: The Apostle
    to Democracy.* New York: The Edward O'Toole Co.,
    1934.
O'Connell, Jeremiah J. *Catholicity in the Carolinas and Georgia.*
    New York: D. and J. Sadlier and Co., 1879.
O'Connell, John, ed. *The Life and Speeches of Daniel O'Connell,
    M.P.* 2 Vols. Dublin: James Duffy, 1846.
    ed. *The Select Speeches of Daniel O'Connell, M.P.* 2
    Vols. Dublin: James Duffy, 1867.
O'Connell, Maurice R. "The Political Background to the Establish-
    ment of Maynooth," *Irish Ecclesiastical Record,* Part I,
    LXXXV (May, 1956), 324-334; Part II, LXXXV (June,
    1956), 406-415; Part III, LXXXVI (July, 1956), 1-16.
    *Irish Politics and Social Conflict in the Age of the
    American Revolution.* Philadelphia: University of Penn-
    sylvania Press, 1965.
    "Daniel O'Connell and Religious Freedom," *The Irish
    Times,* March 4, 1971, p. 18; March 8, 1971, p. 8.
    ed. *Correspondence of Daniel O'Connell.* 8 Vols. Shan-
    non: Irish University Press, 1972-
    "Daniel O'Connell and Religious Freedom." *Thought,* L
    (June, 1975), 176-187.
O'Farrell, Pius. "Francis Moylan, Bishop of Kerry and Cork."
    Unpublished Master's thesis, University College Cork,
    1973.
O'Gorman, Thomas. *A History of the Roman Catholic Church in the
    United States.* Vol. IX: *The American Church History
    Series.* Edited by Philip Schaff *et al.* New York: The
    Christian Literature Co., 1895.
O'Leary, Arthur. *Miscellaneous Tracts.* 2nd ed. Dublin: John
    Chambers, 1781.
Opera Omnia Roberti Cardinalis Bellarmini. 6 vols. Naples:
    Josephum Giuliano, 1856-1862.
O'Shea, John J. *The Two Kenricks.* Philadelphia: John J. McVey,
    1904.
O'Tuathaigh, Gearoid. *Ireland Before the Famine 1798-1848.* Vol. IX
    of *The Gill History of Ireland.* Edited by J. Lydon and
    M. Maccustain. Dublin: Gill and Macmillan Ltd., 1972.
Panczyk, Matthew Leo. "James Whitfield, Fourth Archbishop of
    Baltimore: The Episcopal Years, 1828-1834," Un-
    published Master's thesis, Catholic University of
    America, 1963.

"Papers Relating to the Church in America from the Portfolios of the
Irish College in Rome," *Records of the American
Catholic Historical Society*, VII (1896), 457-487; VIII
(1897), 195-238; 294-329; 450-471.

Reardon, Bernard. *Religious Thought in the Nineteenth Century*.
Cambridge: Cambridge University Press, 1966.

Reynolds, Ignatius A., ed. *The Works of the Right Reverend John
England*. 5 Vols. Baltimore: John Murphy & Co., 1849.

Reynolds, James A. *The Catholic Emancipation Crisis in Ireland,
1823-1829*. New Haven: Yale University Press, 1954.

Roemer, Theodore. *The Catholic Church in the United States*.
St. Louis: B. Herder Book Co., 1950.

Rothensteiner, J. "Bishop England's Correspondence with Bishop
Rosati," *Illinois Catholic Historical Review*, IX (1927)
260-273; 363-371; X(1928) 59-61.

Rousseau, Richard W. "Bishop John England and American Church-
State Theory." Unpublished Ph.D. dissertation, Saint
Paul University, 1969.
"Bishop John England: 1837 Relazione to Rome on his
Haitian Mission," *Archivum Historiae Pontificiae*, XI
(1973), 269-288.
"The Greatness of John England," *American Ecclesi-
astical Review*, CLXVIII (March, 1974), 196-206.

Ruskowski, Leo. *French Emigre Priests in the United States (1791-
1815)*. Vol. XXXII: *The Catholic University of America
Studies in America Church History*. Washington, D. C.:
The Catholic University of America Press, 1940.

Schroeder, Henry J. *Disciplinary Decrees of the General Councils*.
St. Louis: B. Herder Book Co., 1937.

Shaughnessy, Gerald. *Has the Immigrant Kept the Faith? A Study of
Immigration and Catholic Church Growth in the
United States 1790-1920*. New York: Macmillan Co.,
1925.

Shea, John G. *A History of the Catholic Church in the United States*.
4 vols. New York: J. G. Shea, 1886-1892.

Statuta Synodalia Pro Unitis Dioecesibus Cassel et Imelac. . . 1810.
Dublin: Hugo FitzPatrick, 1813.

Storr, V. P. *The Development of English Theology in the Nineteenth
Century 1800-1860*. London: Longmans, Green and
Co., 1913.

Tocqueville, Alexis de. *Democracy in America*. Ed. J. P. Mayer and
Max Lerner; trans. George Lawrence. New York: Haper
and Row, Publishers, 1966.

Torqueblau, P. "Chapitres de chanoines," *Dictionnaire de droit
canoniques* III, 530-95.

Tourscher, Francis E. *The Hogan Schism and Trustee Troubles in St. Mary's Church Philadelphia, 1820-1829.* Philadelphia: Peter Reilly Co., 1930.

Trinterud, Leonard J. *The Forming of an American Tradition: A Re-Examination of Colonial Presbyterianism.* Philadelphia: The Westminster Press, 1949.

Vidler, Alex R. *The Church in an Age of Revolution 1789 to the Present Day.* Grand Rapids, Michigan: Wm. B. Eerdmans Publishing Co., 1961.

Wall, Maureen. *The Penal Laws, 1691-1760: Church and State From the Treaty of Limerick to the Accession of George III.* No. 1: *Irish History Series.* Dundalk, Ireland: Dundalgan Press, 1961.

Walsh, Thomas J. *Nono Nagle and the Presentation Sisters.* Dublin: M. H. Gill and Son Ltd., 1959.

Ward, Bernard. *The Eve of Catholic Emancipation, 1803-1829.* 3 Vols. London: Longmans, Green and Co., 1911-12.

Welch, Claude. *Protestant Thought in the Nineteenth Century.* New Haven: Yale University Press, 1972.

Whyte, John H. "The Influence of the Catholic Clergy on Elections in Nineteenth Century Iréland." *English Historical Review*, LXXV (April, 1960), 239-44.

"The Appointment of Catholic Bishops in Nineteenth Century Ireland," *Catholic Historical Review*, XLVIII (April, 1962), 12-32.

Windele, John. *Historical and Descriptive Notices of Cork.* 2nd ed. Cork: Messrs. Bolster, 1843.

Wittke, Carl F. *The Irish in America.* Baton Rouge, Louisiana: Louisiana State University Press, 1956.

index
